TABE 11 & 12 CONSUMABLE STUDENT READING MANUAL FOR LEVEL E

Preparing Adult Learners for TABE 11 & 12
Reading Tests and for Vocational Training and College
Entrance Reading Exams

By Coaching for Better Learning, LLC

TABE 11 & 12
CONSUMABLE STUDENT
READING MANUAL
FOR LEVEL E

*Preparing Adult Learners
for TABE 11 & 12 Reading Tests &
Vocational Training and College
Entrance Reading Exams*

BY COACHING FOR BETTER LEARNING, LLC

TABLE OF CONTENTS

INTRODUCTION

This student reading manual prepares adult learners for the TABE 11 & 12 Level E reading test and vocational training admission reading tests. In other words, it presents exercises that help adult education and workforce programs and their learners meet the Workforce Innovation and Opportunity Act (WIOA) reading expectations.

The reading exercises and answer keys of this manual cover TABE 11 & 12 Level E and CCR reading standards and content. For example, the reading comprehension exercises address

- **Phonics and word recognition.**
- **Key ideas and details.**
- **Craft and structure.**
- **Integration of knowledge and ideas.**

The manual is divided into 18 sections as follows:

Lesson 1: Suggestions for Better Reading Comprehension
Lesson 2: Developing Phonemic Awareness
Lesson 3: Building Decoding Skills
Lesson 4: Using Background Knowledge
Lesson 5: Making Inferences and Predictions
Lesson 6: Using Visual Imagery
Lesson 7: Building Vocabulary and Using Context Clues
Lesson 8: Understanding Question-Answer Relationships
Lesson 9: Learning Non-Fiction Text Features
Lesson 10: Reading for Main Ideas
Lesson 11: Understanding What You Read
Lesson 12: Using Text Structure to Build Reading Comprehension
Lesson 13: Understanding Point of View
Lesson 14: How to Read Maps, Charts and Data Tables
Lesson 15: Reading Long Passages
Reading Skills Self-Evaluation
Practice Tests
Answer Keys

Learning phonemic awareness skills will help you decode words and build your vocabulary. But reading is more than decoding and pronouncing the words. Reading is understanding what you read and making meaning.

Therefore, this manual is designed for adult learners as an instructional guide for developing reading comprehension strategies and skills. The book offers reading strategies to help adult learners become more active, strategic and purposeful readers. These strategies will also help learners understand and remember what they read.

Reading is an active thinking process. Therefore, this book encourages learners to actively engage with texts by predicting, making connections and inferences, asking and answering questions, and completing comprehension activities.

Reading Strategies

The strategies taught in this manual are all based on the research on teaching reading. These strategies are

- *Developing Phonemic Awareness.*
- *Building Decoding Skills.*
- *Using Background Knowledge.*
- *Making Inferences and Predictions.*
- *Using Visual Imagery.*
- *Building Vocabulary Using Context Clues.*
- *Understanding Question-Answer Relationships (QARs).*
- *Learning Non-Fiction Text Features.*
- *Reading for Main Ideas.*
- *Understanding What You Read.*
- *Using Text Structure to Build Reading Comprehension.*
- *Understanding Point of View.*
- *How to Read Graphs and Data.*

Examples of the different strategies are provided in the first section of the manual. After the lessons and examples, the manual provides practice exercises for using the strategies for longer passages.

All the reading strategies are presented with examples, pictures and text. These learning aids will give you hands-on practice and help you understand each strategy and how it works. As you read, study and work through these examples, you will build the confidence to succeed. **You will become a strategic reader**. Let's get started!

LESSON 1

SUGGESTIONS FOR BETTER READING COMPREHENSION

Students who learn to be strategic, purposeful readers can use reading strategies to gain access to any type of text. To learn to be a purposeful reader, follow these steps:

Read about the strategy.

Examine the particular strategy you are about to learn by looking at the **title or topic** of the lesson. Study the pictures and any other illustrations. Doing these will prepare you for learning the strategy.

Use your background knowledge.

We all have background knowledge on many subjects. When you begin each reading lesson, **think about what you know** about the topic.

- Use the topic and pictures to guess what the lesson will be about.
- Ask yourself, "What do I know about this topic or subject?"
- Ask questions about the text and the author.
- Link the subject matter to similar topics you have read about and your world knowledge.

Read the directions carefully.

Study each reading skill by reading the directions. Pay attention to the process, examples and exercises. They will build your understanding of how the strategy is used.	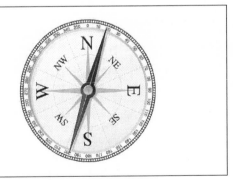

Practice the strategy.

Read and practice. Read about the strategy and practice it in your personal and academic readings. This will help you get better and better.

Re-read the passages.

Where there are passages, re-read them, pause to answer questions, think through the information and draw conclusions.

Increase your vocabulary.

Use context clues or a dictionary to decode words you may not understand.

Respond.

Read the passages over and over. Continual reading and practice will help each strategy you learn become automatic for you.

Read regularly and study reading strategies.

- You will improve your reading skills by reading regularly for work or pleasure and studying reading strategies that proficient readers use. For example, you should

    ⇒ Learn the types of questions you might be asked while reading.
    ⇒ Practice identifying different types of texts and their structures.
    ⇒ Learn to identify main ideas, topic sentences, main arguments and supporting details in your reading texts.
    ⇒ Get used to identifying the author's purpose or the intent of the passage you are reading.
    ⇒ Learn to skim-read texts for general information or an overview.
    ⇒ Practice scanning texts for specific information or details.
    ⇒ Learn to infer or deduct what the author does not say explicitly.
    ⇒ Learn to find evidence from a text that refutes or supports an argument.
    ⇒ Keep working on increasing your reading speed by moving your eyes across the page and focusing on content words or groups of words instead of reading and sounding out one word at a time.
    ⇒ Try to summarize each paragraph you read. The more you use this practice, the better you will get at comprehending and retaining information.

	You will become a successful reader.

REFLECTION ON LEARNING

Answer the following reflection questions, and feel free to discuss your responses with your teacher or classmate.

- What reading idea or strategy did you learn from this section?

- What new concepts did you learn?

- What methods did you work on in this section?

- What aspect of this section is still not 100 percent clear for you?

- What do you want your teacher to know?

LESSON 2

DEVELOPING PHONEMIC AWARENESS

How can phonemic awareness help you become a better reader?

What are phonemes? Phonemes are the smallest units of sound in a spoken language, and English has 44 of them. There are 26 letters in the alphabet, but there are 44 different sounds. These 44 sounds fall into two categories: vowels **(a, e, i, o, u)** and consonants **(b, c, d, f, g, h, j, k, l, m, n, p, q, r, s, t, v, w, x, y, z)**. Vowels and consonants give us the spoken sounds of English.

There are 5 vowel letters but 20 vowel phonemes or sounds. There are 21 consonants but 24 consonant (and digraph) phonemes or sounds. Phonemes are usually written between slashes. For example, /a/ and /e/.

Short and Long Vowels

Long vowels say their own names, and we hold them longer than short vowels when we speak.

Below are some examples of **short-vowel and long-vowel phonemes**.

Short vowel /a/ 'a' as in <u>cat</u>		Long vowels /a/ 'a' as in <u>cake</u>	
/e/ 'e' as in <u>egg</u>		Long/e/ 'e' as in she	

Short vowel /i/ 'i' as in Pig		Long vowel /i/ /i/ as in kite	
Short vowel /o/ 'o' as in jog		Long vowel /o/ /o/ as in snow	
Short vowel /u/ 'u' as in umbrella		Long /u/ /u/ as in cube ice cubes	

Read the examples, write down your observations and discuss them with a classmate.

Examples of Short and Long Vowels

Short /a/	Long /a/	Short /e/	Long /e/
Can	Cane *(silent e)*	Bed	Be
Back	Bake	Shed	She
Plan	Plane	Met	Me
Rat	Rate	Wet	We, He, Me
Snack	Snake		

Short /i/	Long /i/	Short /o/	Long /o/
Hid	Hide	Hop	Hope
Slid	Slide	Rob	Robe
Dim	Dime	Cot	Phone
Bit	Bite	Rot	Wrote
Fin	Fine		

Short /u/ and Long /u/

C<u>u</u>b	C<u>u</u>be
H<u>u</u>g	H<u>u</u>ge
C<u>u</u>t	C<u>u</u>te
T<u>u</u>b	T<u>u</u>be

Answer these questions with a partner.

1- What role does ***the silent e*** play in the words with long vowel sounds? Discuss with a classmate.

2- What happens when you remove ***the silent e*** from these words*: Rate, Plane, Cute, Site* and *Tube?* Discuss with a classmate.

The Silent "e" Rule

When a vowel and a consonant are followed by one "e," the "e" is almost always silent, but the vowel before it is long.

Example: ate, bite, nine, cube

> **Rule 1:** A vowel at the end of a syllable is almost always _long_.
> Examples: we, he, she, potato, hero
>
> **Rule 2:** The vowel /e/ at the end of a multi-syllable word is almost always _silent_.
> Examples: female, terminate, dictate, sentence, possessive, practice

EXERCISE 1
Read this passage and complete the exercises below.

Yes, she knew she must go back to all that, but at present she must <u>weep</u>. <u>Screening</u> her face, she sobbed more steadily than she had yet done, her shoulders rising and falling with great <u>regularity</u>. It was this figure that her husband saw when, having reached the polished Sphinx, having <u>entangled</u> himself with a man selling picture postcards, he turned; the stanza <u>instantly</u> stopped. He came up to her, laid his hand on her shoulder, and said, "Dearest." His voice was supplicating. But she shut her face away from him, as much as to say, "You can't possibly understand."

Excerpt from The Voyage Out by Virginia Woolf (1882-1941)

1- Complete the table with words from the text and compare with a partner. For example, some words with <u>short /e/ sounds</u> are **spell** and **energy.**

Short /e/	Short /a/	Short /o/	Long /i/	Long /a/
spell				

2- What is happening in this passage?

3- What are the meanings of the <u>underlined</u> words? Discuss them with a classmate.

4- Write a title for the passage and compare your answer with a partner's.

5- Read the following sentence: *Yes, she knew she must go back to all that, but at present she must weep.*
Based on this sentence, what do you know about the person who is weeping?

R-Controlled Vowels

If a vowel is followed by "r," the "r" changes the vowel's sound into a different sound.

Examples:

- "ar" almost always makes the same sound.
- "or" almost always makes the same sound.
- "ir", "ur" and "er" make the same sounds almost always.

AR	OR	IR	UR	ER
Bar	For	Bird	Fur	Her
Car	Corn	Dirt	Blurt	Fern
Far	Storm	Skirt	Burp	Stern
Farm	Fork	Squirt	Hurt	Verb
Barn	Born	Third	Curl	Term
Start	Horn	Firm	Surf	Super
Park	Lord	Girl	Lurk	Mother
Shark	Word	Whirl	Turn	Swerve
Lark			Burn	Ever

What Is a Diphthong?

A diphthong is a combination of two vowel sounds into a different sound. The sound begins as one vowel and moves or glides towards another. Say the words below and pay attention to the sounds in the diphthongs /oi/, /oy/, /ou/ and /ow/.

oi	oy	ou	ow
noise	joy	cloud	cow
voice	boy	south	bow
soil	toys	south	plow
join	enjoy	mouth	how
coin	destroy	mouse	wow

What Are Vowel Digraphs?

Vowel digraphs are vowels (including w and y) that combine to make a single sound or a diphthong. Look at these examples:

oa	ai	ee	ea	oo	oo	ow	ew	ou	aw
boat	rain	bee	sea	zoo	book	cow	new	cloud	law
coat	brain	eel	tea	food	look	clown	chew	mouse	saw
loaf	chain	seed	leaf	moon	cook	towel	crew	count	jaw
soap	train	sheep	teach	tooth	hook	town	dew	loud	yawn
road	main	teeth	beach	booth	foot	brown	stew	mouth	claw

EXERCISE 2

Read this passage and complete the exercises below.

Mrs. Chailey was expected to sit in a cabin which was large enough, but too near the boilers, so that after five minutes, she could hear her heart "go," she <u>complained,</u> putting her hand above it, which was a <u>state</u> of things that Mrs. Vinrace, Rachel's mother, would never have dreamt of <u>inflicting</u>—Mrs. Vinrace, who <u>knew</u> every sheet in her house, and <u>expected</u> of every one the best they could do, but no more.

Excerpt from The Voyage Out by Virginia Woolf (1882-1941)

1- Complete the table with words from the text and compare your answers with a partner's. For example, a word with the "ar" sound is **large.**

Sound /oi/	Sound /ea/	Sound /ee/	Sound /er/	Sound /ar/
				Large

2- What is happening in this passage?

3- What are the meanings of the <u>underlined</u> words? Discuss your answers with a classmate.

4- Write a title for the passage and compare your answer with a partner's.

5- Based on the passage, what do you know about Mrs. Vinrace?

Consonants Clusters and Consonant Blends

Consonant Clusters	Consonant Blends
When two or three consonants appear together, they form a *consonant cluster.* Example: <u>ST</u> in the word STAR The term **cluster** refers to the written form.	The term *blend* refers to the spoken form or the sound formed by consonant clusters. Each consonant keeps its own sound. Each **sound is heard in the blend**. *See the examples in the table below.*

Consonant clusters can be in the <u>beginning</u>, <u>middle</u> or <u>end</u> of words.

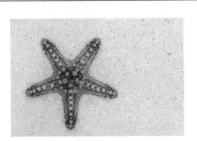 /st/ **Beginning consonant cluster**	s+ t = /st/ **star** – Consonant cluster /st/ The consonant cluster /st/ is at the <u>beginning</u> of the word "st**ar**."
 /st / **Middle consonant cluster**	**oysters** – Consonant cluster /st / The consonant cluster /st / is in the <u>middle</u> of the word "cluster."
 /st/ **Ending consonant cluster**	**fist** – Consonant cluster /st/ The consonant cluster /st/ is at the <u>end</u> of the word "fi**st**."

Why should you study phonological awareness?

Phonological awareness helps you let go of focusing on the letters in words and **focus on the sounds** in the spoken words instead.

Blender: /bl/ consonant blend

There are six "L-blends":

Be careful to say the **sounds** of the letters together and not each of their names.

Here are some words that have L-blends:

/bl/ - blog, black, blend, bless, blot

/cl/ - clap, club, class, clock

/fl/ - flag, flap, flow, flute, flower

/gl/ - glass, glad, globe

/pl/ - plan, plate, plot, plug, plane

/sl/ - slip, slippers, slow, slam, slacks

EXERCISE 3

1. Look at the picture below.

What is the beginning **consonant blend** of the word represented in the picture?

A. /st/
B. /gl/
C. /fl/
D. /cl/

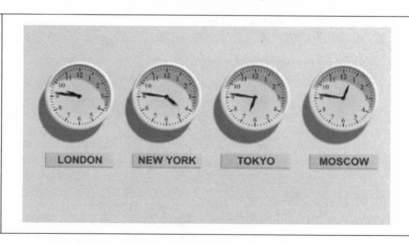

R-blends are consonant blends that include the letter "**r**." "**R**" is the second letter in an r-blend. Be careful to say the **sounds** of the letters together and not their individual names:

 Crab: /cr/ consonant blend	There are **seven r-blends:** /br/ - brick, brave, bridge, brain /cr/ - crab, crisp, crazy, cry /dr/ - drop, draw, dream, dress /fr/ - frog, fresh, frozen, frighten /gr/ - grapes, grass, grow, great /pr/ - pram, prove, prone, promise /tr/ - train, trade, travel, tree

2.   Look at the picture.

What is the beginning **consonant blend** of the word represented by the object in the picture? A. /pr/ B. /br/ C. /tr/ D. /cr/	 Remember that blends are two letters that make two sounds. **The sounds are blended.**

S-blends are consonant blends that include the letter "s," which is the first letter in an s-blend. Be careful to say the sounds of the letters together and not their individual names. **Remember that blends are two letters that make two sounds.**

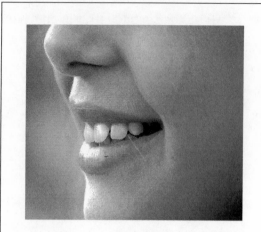

Smile: /sm/ consonant blend

There are seven /s/ blends:

/sk/ - skate, ski, skeleton, skin, sky

/sl/ - slide, slim, slick, slam, slow

/sm/ - smile, small, smart, smell

/sn/ - snake, snack, snore, snail

/sp/ - spot, spider, speak, spend, sport

/st/ step, stick, stop, star, stone

/sw/ swam, sweet, swim, swing, sweat

3. Look at the picture.

1. **Say the blend**.
2. **Say the word** for the picture.
3. **Write a sentence** about each picture.

Remember, blends are two letters that make two sounds.

SW - **Swimmer**

SK - **Skater**

GR - **Grapes**

BL - **Block**

4. **Write 5 words that have each of the following blends.**

R-blend: _____

L-blend: _____

S- blend: _____

18

Consonant Blends at the End of Words

There are more consonant blends than the ones previously discussed, but they occur <u>mostly at the end</u> of words. These ending blends include -st, -sk, -sp, -nt, -nk, -rk, -lt, -lf, -ft, -nd, -mp, -rd, -ld.

Say the following words:

-st	-sk	-sp	-nt	-nk
best	ask	clasp	parent	bank
fast	desk	crisp	plant	drink
just	disk	grasp	student	junk
last	dusk	lisp	want	pink
lost	mask	wasp	went	thank
must	risk	wisp		think
rest	task			

-rk	-lt	-lf	-ft	-nd
ark	adult	calf	craft	and
irk	belt	half	gift	band
jerk	fault	elf	left	land
park	melt	golf	lift	stand
work	salt	self	soft	end
	tilt	wolf		bend
				send

Here are some more consonant blends. Say the following words:

Words ending in **/mp/** – camp, damp, jump, lamp, pump, stamp, dump
Words ending in **/rd/** – bird, card, hard, record, word, yard
Words ending in **/ld/** – cold, fold, gold, hold, mold

Example of a consonant blend at the beginning and end: STAMP

ST	A	MP	

Exercise 4

Read this passage and complete the exercises below.

> In March 1979, Voyager 1 <u>swept</u> past Jupiter, photographing both the giant planet and five of its moons. Four months later, a companion <u>spacecraft</u>, Voyager 2, made a similar <u>encounter</u>. Now, with Jupiter <u>receding</u> behind them, both spacecraft are headed toward the outer reaches of our solar system. In November 1980, Voyager 1 will fly past Saturn. Voyager 2, traveling at slower speeds, will reach the same way station in August 1981. Beyond there, the <u>itinerary</u> is less certain. In January 1986, eight years after its departure from Earth, Voyager 2 may sail within range of Uranus, taking closeup pictures of that distant planet for the first time. Long after they have <u>exhausted</u> their fuel supplies and their radios have fallen silent, both spacecraft will continue their traverse through space and beyond our solar system, on an <u>endless</u> journey.
>
> _____
> Excerpt from Voyager Encounters Jupiter by National Aeronautics and Space Administration

1- Complete the table with words from the text and compare your answers with a partner's. For example, a word with an r-blend is "**spacecraft**."

R-blend	S-blend	L-blend	Long /e/	Long /a/

2- What is happening in this passage?
3- What's the meaning of the <u>underlined</u> words? Discuss them with a classmate.
4- Write a title for the passage and compare your answer with a partner's.

5- **Write 3 words that end with each of the following blends or sounds.**

ST_____

SP_____

Three-Letter Blends

There are also **three-letter blends**. These are mostly found at the beginning of words.

Examples:
s + t + r = /str/ as in str-eet
s + c + r = /scr/ as in scr-eam

Be sure to say the sound of the letters together and not their individual names.

More Three-Letter /s/ Blends

Scr– scrap, scratch, scrawl, scream, screw, script, scrub

Shr – shrimp, shrink, shrine, shrub, shrug

Spl– splash, spleen, splendid, splinter, splice, split

Spr – spray, sprain, spread, spring, sprint,

Squ – squad, square, squash, squish, squeeze, squib, squirrel, squirt

Str – stranger, strap, straw, streak, stream, street, strength, stretch, string, strong

Below are some three-letter words beginning with the blend /thr/. Sound them out and say the words:

thread	threaten
three	thrill
throne	through
throw	throb

Say the word in the picture below. Pay attention to the ending blend "**mp.**" Circle all the words that end with the same sound in the box below.

bump	clump	
hump	string	
plump	thump	
thumb	lip	
dump	dip	
lump	welcome	
		Jump

Having Three Consonant Blends in One Word

In the word *smashing* (**sm**- a - **sh**- i- **ng**), there are three consonant blends. This example shows you how important consonant blends are in learning to read.

Consonant Digraphs (Beginning Position)

A digraph consists of two letters that come together to make one sound.

In the following consonant digraph, two consonants **make one sound** when blended. The most common consonant digraphs are sh, ch, th, wh, ph, ng, wr and ck

Digraphs in the Beginning Position

sh	sheep, ship, shake, shop, sheet, she, shout, shiny, shell
ch	chair, check, chain, child, chart, chime, chalk
th	thorn, that, them, thick, thief, thirsty, thump, thumb, thick
ph	phone, phrase, phobia, phoneme, pharmacy, physical
wh	whale, what, wheat, wheel, which, whip, white, whisper
wr	wrong, write, wrap, wreck, wring, wreath, wrist

Digraphs in the Ending

sh	gosh, cash, rash, wash, brush, posh, fish
ch	each, rich, inch, bench, touch, coach, catch, lunch, match
th	mouth, south, earth, tooth, cloth, moth, math, youth
ck	shack, stack, slick, shock, speech, black, block
ng	bang, fang, gang, hang, sang,
ph	graph, digraph, trophy

Example of a digraph at the end: FI**SH**

F	I	**SH**

The digraph "sh" makes one sound.

The Consonant Digraph "ng"

Words may end with the digraph "ng" or may have the digraph "ng" in them. Very often, "ng" is part of the suffix "-ing."

• Gang	• Ding
• Hang	• Thing
• Rang	• Ring
• Sang	• Sing
• Bang	• Bring
• Song	• Singing
• Long	• Bringing
• Wrong	• Zinging

Exercise 5

Can you think of two other words that contain the digraph "ng"?

1. _____

2. _____

Below are some examples of the consonant digraphs "ph" in the **middle position**:

ph	alphabet, prophet, hyphen, nephew, typhoon, orphan, dolphin

PRACTICE EXERCISE

Read this passage and complete the exercises below.

> Deep into that darkness peering, long I stood there <u>wondering</u>, fearing,
> Doubting, dreaming dreams no <u>mortal</u> ever <u>dared</u> to dream before;
> But the silence was unbroken, and the <u>stillness</u> gave no token,
> And the only word there spoken was the <u>whispered</u> word, "Lenore!"
> This I whispered, and an <u>echo</u> murmured back the word, "Lenore!"—
> Merely this and nothing more.
>
> _____
>
> Excerpt from The Raven by Edgar Allan Poe

1- What is happening in this passage?

2- What's the meaning of the <u>underlined</u> words? Discuss with a classmate.

3- Write a title for the poem and compare your answer with a partner's.

4- Write 4 words with the following sounds, then compare your answers with a classmate's.

sh_____

ch_____

th_____

ph_____

The words below have the same sound: /K/.

C:	cat, coat, cut, cake, cute, cold, call, culture, college,
K:	kite, kit, kill, keen, keep, kind, kick, keel

5- Read the above lists carefully. When should you use <u>c</u> and <u>k</u> to make the sound /k/? Discuss your observation with a partner's.

REFLECTION ON LEARNING

Answer the following reflection questions, and feel free to discuss your responses with your teacher or classmate.

- What reading idea or strategy did you learn from this section?

- What new concepts did you learn?

- What methods did you work on in this section?

- What aspect of this section is still not 100 percent clear for you?

- What do you want your teacher to know?

LESSON 3
BUILDING DECODING SKILLS

Word Families

A word family is a group of words that have a similar pattern. Some families have the same combination of letters or the same sound. Studying word families can help you build vocabulary and spelling skills. It can also assist you in learning to sound out words and decode.

| Word Families Example:

-**ay**, as in s<u>ay</u> and pl<u>ay</u>	

When you learn to recognize a word pattern, you can use your prior knowledge of the word family to decode new words. You can then learn related words like

- Play**ing**
- Play**er**
- Play**ed**
- Play**s**

Read the following word family. Say the words.

Meet the "-ad" family. Some members of the family are

mad	sad	bad	had	pad	lad

Exercise 1

1. **Below are other word families. Underline all the long /a/ sounds and compare your answers with a partner's.**

-at	-ate	-ap	-ash
bat	date	cap	brash
cat	gate	flap	crash
hat	grate	gap	dash
mat	plate	lap	flash
rat	rate	map	rash
sat	state	trap	smash

2. **Underline all the verbs and compare your answer with a partner's.**

-in	-it	-ing	-ill
bin	bit	cling	bill
chin	fit	fling	drill
fin	hit	king	hill
gin	knit	ring	mill
grin	pit	sing	pill
skin	quit	thing	skill
thin	split	wring	still

3.

-ink	-ip	-ain	-ay
blink	chip	brain	bay
drink	dip	chain	clay
link	drip	drain	day
pink	flip	gain	delay
rink	grip	main	gray
sink	hip	pain	may
stink	lip	rain	okay
think	ship		play

Exercise 2

All the words in a family rhyme with one another. Write 4 other words in each word family below.

-ack	-eat	-ice	-ick
black	eat	dice	brick
hack	beat	mice	chick
pack	cheat	nice	flick
quack	heat	price	kick

Exercise 3

Below are more word families.

1. **Say** each word.
2. **Write** it in the air with your finger.
3. **Visualize it.** Whether it is a noun or verb, take a picture for your imagination.
4. Choose 7 words from the table below and write a sentence with each.

-all	-ame	-op	-oke
ball	blame	chop	broke
call	came	crop	choke
fall	fame	drop	joke
hall	frame	hop	poke
mall	game	mop	spoke
tall	name	pop	woke

Choose 7 words from the table below, read them and discuss their meanings with a classmate.

-an	-ide	-ore	-ank
ban	bride	bore	bank
can	hide	chore	blank
fan	ride	more	crank
man	side	score	drank
pan	slide	sore	plank
ran	tide	store	sank

Practice Task

Write the words you cannot read in these word families on **3x5 cards**. Try to read them. Spell them. Use each one of them in a sentence.

-ight	-ot	-ake	-ell
bright	blot	bake	bell
fright	cot	cake	dwell
height	dot	fake	fell
right	hot	make	sell
sight	knot	rake	shell
light	lot	snake	smell
	spot	take	tell

Exercise 4

1. Choose 5 words from the table below. Use them in sentences and discuss their meanings with a classmate.

-ump	-aw	-uck	-ug
bump	claw	cluck	bug
clump	draw	duck	hug
dump	flaw	pluck	jug
jump	jaw	stuck	mug
plump	law	truck	shrug
stump	paw	tuck	snug
	saw		

2. Choose 5 words from the table below. Use them in sentences and discuss their meanings with a classmate.

-ale	-est	- ock
bale	best	block
gale	chest	clock
kale	crest	dock
male	nest	flock
pale	pest	lock
scale	rest	rock
stale	test	sock

Practice Task

Mix up your 3x5 word cards from the previous activity. Then sort the cards into piles based on word families.

Building Decoding Skills

Prefixes, Suffixes and Base Words

A *prefix* is placed at the beginning of a word. A *suffix* is placed at the end of a word. In the middle is the **root** or the **stem**.

Example:

Look at the word "impossible." The root "possible" means something can happen. The prefix "im-" means "no" or "not." So the word "impossible" means *not possible*. **If you learn common prefixes, suffixes and roots, you will be able to decode many unknown words.**

Common Prefixes

Prefix	Meaning	Example	Base/Root
Dis-	not	**dis**like	like
Im-	not	**im**possible	possible
In-	not	**in**active	active
Mis-	wrong	**mis**take	take
Pre-	before	**pre**pay	pay
Re-	back, again	**re**do	do
Un-	not	**un**tie	tie

Exercise 5

Look at each sentence and then complete the word below.

The rude girl was very _____ to the teacher.

   A. Not polite – im_____

There is a lot of crime in the city, so I feel _____.

   B. Not safe – un_____

I did my homework last night, but it had a lot of mistakes. So, I need to _____ it.

   C. do again – re_____

The boy behaved badly at the doctor's office. He _____ .

   D. Behave badly – mis_____

28

Common Suffixes

Suffix	Meaning	Example	Base/root
-er, -or	the person doing the action	read-er, invent-or, teach-er	read, invent, teach
-est	the most	wis-est, happi - est	wise, happy
-less	without	home-less	home
-ing	in the act of doing something	walk-ing	walk
-ly	the characteristic of something	soft-ly, slow-ly, happ-ily	soft, slow, happy
-ful	full of; characterized by	play-ful, skill-ful	play, skill
-ant	one who is or does	claim-ant	claim

Exercise 6

1. Add **–ed** and **–ing** to each word in the table. Write the new words on the lines.

Example: drop, dropping, dropped

Note: Some root words or base words can change because of their prefixes and suffixes. For example, "drop" gets another "p" in "dropping" and "dropped."

Word	Add *-ed*	Add *-ing*
Rub	a. _____	b. _____
Fix	c. _____	d. _____
Jog	e. _____	f. _____
Hop	g. _____	h. _____
Pick	i. _____	j. _____

2. **Read this poem one more time and complete the table below.**

> Deep into that darkness peering, long I stood there wondering, fearing,
> Doubting, dreaming dreams no mortal ever dared to dream before;
> But the silence was unbroken, and the stillness gave no token,
> And the only word there spoken was the whispered word, "Lenore!"
> This I whispered, and an echo murmured back the word, "Lenore!"—
> Merely this and nothing more.
>
> Excerpt from "The Raven" by Edgar Allan Poe

Complete the table with words from the passage that have prefixes or suffixes. Discuss their meanings with a classmate.

Words with Prefixes	Words with Suffixes

Syllabication: Dividing Words into Their Syllables

Words have different sound parts. When you divide a word into its sound parts or <u>syllables,</u> you can **blend the sound parts** and say the word. You can also break up long words into syllables and say them easily.

Each syllable should have a vowel sound. The number of vowel sounds tends to be the number of syllables, but there might be exceptions.

Ask yourself:

1. How many vowel sounds do I hear? (Silent **e** does not count.)
2. Are the vowels together or apart?
3. How many syllables are there?

Words	Number of Vowels		Number of Vowel Sounds	Number of Syllables	
all	1	A	1	1	all
number	2	U E	2	2	num-ber
Bahamas	3	A A A	3	3	Ba-ha-mas
America	4	A E I A	4	4	A-mer-i-ca
fantastic	3	A A I	3	3	fan-tas-tic
repeating	4	E E A I	3	3	re-peat-ing
establish	3	E A I	3	3	es-tab-lish

One Vowel

The words below have **one vowel sound**. What rule applies to words with one vowel sound?

are, an, and, as, at, get, now, on, one, than, they, who, what, when

Rule 1: Words with one vowel sound have one syllable.

Two Vowels

The words below have **two vowels**. What rule applies to words with two vowel sounds?

rock-et, din-ner, lum-ber, chick-en, rob-ber, jack-et, can-dy, lit-tle, num-ber, mon-ster

Rule 2: Words with two vowel sounds have two syllables.

Three Vowels

The words below have three vowels. What rule applies to words with three vowel sounds?

add-i-tion, a-ni-mal, a-ssem-ble, a-tten-dance, a-ttrac-tion, be-ginn-ing, cha-rac-ter, dis-cov-er

Rule 3: Words with three vowel sounds have three syllables.

Exceptions to the Rule

Vowel teams are two vowels that make one sound.

We divide between two vowels if both have separate sounds but not if they make only one sound together. For example, we divide between the two vowels in "di-a-meter" but not in "found."

Examples of Vowel Teams:

/ee/ - bee, peel, feet, weed, peek, feed
/ea/ - beak, leap, tea, team, meat, read, beach
/ey/ - jersey, turkey, valley, honey, money
/ai/ - sail, tail, nail, rain, train, faint

Rule 4: Divide before the consonant if a word has a single consonant between two vowels.

Example: ti-ger, fi-ber

However, this does not always work, so sound out the word to figure out if it makes sense.

Rule 5: If a consonant is between two vowels, divide **before** the consonant if the first vowel has the **long** sound and **after** the consonant if the first vowel is **short** and accented.

Example: ti-ger, fi-ber, cab-in

Rule 6: Divide double consonants in the middle unless they form a digraph.

Example: sil-ly, let-ter, mar-ble, plas-ma, Eas-ter

Consonant digraphs are the exception to this rule. Remember that digraphs are two consonants *that make one sound. For example, we say rath-er, not rat-her, and tel-e-phone not tel- ep-hone)*

Rule 7: Learn the special rule about *-le* words.

Words that end in a consonant plus *le* must be divided **before** the consonant and *-le* pattern.

Examples: bub-ble, ma-ple, pur-ple

However, if the **ck** digraph comes before *-le*, *ck* cannot be separated.

Examples: pick-le, buck-le

Rule 8: Divide compound words between the two base words.

The two words in a compound word each has a meaning, for example, *wall* and *paper* of "wallpaper" and *drive* and *way* of "driveway." To divide into syllables, first divide the compound word between its base parts: wall-paper. Since *paper* has two vowels, the syllables are wall-pa-per.

Strategy: Use clapping when saying the words.

If you think you know the number of syllables but you are not sure, clap for each syllable.

book (one clap)

farm-er (two claps)

gas-o-line (three claps)

trans-por-ta-tion (four claps)

(You can also try drumming or touching your chin when saying the words.)

PRACTICE EXERCISE

Break the words below into syllables. After, look up their meanings and discuss them with a classmate.

Words	Syllables (Sound Parts)
1- Lumber	Lum - ber
2- College	
3- Analysis	
4- University	
5- Specific	
6- Area	
7- Management	
8- Assessment	
9- Enrollment	
10- Application	
11- Tuition	
12- Response	
13- Informative	
14- Professor	
15- Academy	
16- Economic	
17- Library	
18- Composition	
19- Dissertation	
20- Research	
21- Environment	
22- Interpretation	
23- Method	
24- Policy	
25- Procedure	
26- Theory	
27- Significant	

COACHING FOR BETTER LEARNING

REFLECTION ON LEARNING

Answer the following reflection questions, and feel free to discuss your responses with your teacher or classmate.

- What reading idea or strategy did you learn from this section?

- What new concepts did you learn?

- What methods did you work on in this section?

- What aspect of this section is still not 100 percent clear for you?

- What do you want your teacher to know?

LESSON 4

USING BACKGROUND KNOWLEDGE

By the end of this lesson, you will be able to use your background knowledge when reading a text. Using your background knowledge is an important reading strategy that can help you understand what you read.

1) When you use background knowledge, you think of how the **text relates to you**. You use your personal experience to help make meaning of the reading.

For example, if you are reading a passage about vacation spots, you can think of places you visited while on vacation. You can reflect on that time when you climbed up a mountain, swam in a lake, explored a cave, went to a big city, or so on. In this way, you are using your knowledge, or **text-to-self knowledge.**

Text-to-Self You make a connection between a text you are reading and something in your own life. Ask yourself, "What does this reading remind me of in my own life?"	

2) When reading a book or other text, you should also think of how it **relates to other books** you have read or movies you have seen. Perhaps you have read several books by the same author. Perhaps you have read another article on the same subject.

For example, let's say you are reading a text about US history. Immediately, you think, "Oh, yes, I used to read or watch movies about this topic." You remember information about the Revolutionary War, British colonization, slavery and Independence Day. You then start to guess what the text will be about. Doing this gives you a **mindset** for reading. **Using your prior knowledge** might help you understand and learn new information faster.

Text-to-Text You make a connection between a text you are reading and something you read or saw before. Ask yourself, "Have I read about this topic before? What do I already know about it?"	

3) When you are reading, you should also connect the text to ideas and events in the world. As an adult, you have a **great deal of world knowledge**. You acquired this huge amount of information throughout your life.

You gathered it from the books you read and studied, and from the various media sources like the Internet, TV, radio, and so on. Of course, you also gathered information from your family, friends, teachers, and all the others with whom you associate. So, you should draw on this knowledge to help you understand what you read better.

Text-to-World

You connect a text you are reading with all your knowledge about the world.

Ask yourself, "What does this remind me of in the world?"

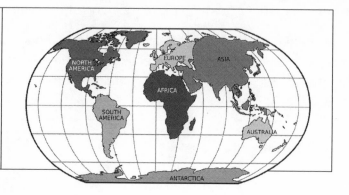

PRACTICE EXERCISE

Read this passage another time and answer the question below.

> Deep into that darkness peering, long I stood there wondering, fearing,
> Doubting, dreaming dreams no mortal ever dared to dream before;
> But the silence was unbroken, and the stillness gave no token,
> And the only word there spoken was the whispered word, "Lenore!"
> This I whispered, and an echo murmured back the word, "Lenore!"—
> Merely this and nothing more.
>
> _____
> Excerpt from "The Raven" by Edgar Allan Poe

Answer these questions about the passage.

1. What comes to your mind when you read this text?

   _____

2. How can you connect the text with the world around you?

   _____

REFLECTION ON LEARNING

Answer the following reflection questions, and feel free to discuss your responses with your teacher or classmate.

- What reading idea or strategy did you learn from this section?

- What new concepts did you learn?

- What methods did you work on in this section?

- What aspect of this section is still not 100 percent clear for you?

- What do you want your teacher to know?

LESSON 5

MAKING INFERENCES AND PREDICTIONS

By the end of this lesson, you will be able to make inferences based on

- observations.
- pictures.
- text and data.

What is an inference?

As a reader, you need to make *inferences* to understand what you read. An inference is an "educated guess." The examples that follow should help you understand inferences and how to infer as you read.

A. You can make inferences based on observations.

Scenario 1

Imagine you are in line at the bank to make a withdrawal. There are four persons ahead of you. One is a fairly young man in his late 20s. He has a beard and hat, and he keeps looking around before getting to the teller. When he gets to the teller, he hands her a note and her expression changes suddenly. Her eyes open wide, her hands begin to shake, and she looks surprised and shocked.

What do you infer? Circle <u>each</u> answer you think is true.

A. He passed her a note for money. He must be a bank robber.
B. She is terrified of what he could do as he is young.

Scenario 2

You have been away on vacation and get back one week earlier than planned. You live alone but return to find your car is not parked in your driveway where you left it.

Circle the <u>best</u> inference.

A. My neighbor moved my car.
B. My brother borrowed my car.
C. Maybe I forgot where I parked.

Scenario 3

You are Jabari's mom, and he has his first soccer game. He is dressed up and ready to take the field. You and your spouse are in the stands, very eager to see him play. The coach whistles for players to take their positions. However, Jabari stays frozen on the sidelines.

Exercise 1
Identify then circle the <u>best</u> inference.

A. Jabari might be sick.
B. Jabari is nervous.
C. Jabari does not want to play anymore.
D. Jabari is lazy.

Are you beginning to understand inferences now? You **view the situation or read** the text, you **think of prior knowledge** of the situation or context, and you **make an educated guess**. It is that simple!

B. You can also make inferences based on pictures.

Picture 1 – Rose petals in front of a church	Picture 2 – A lonely fisherman

Picture 3: The boy and the shark	Picture 4: A cat near a tree looking scared

Exercise 2
Use your prior knowledge and the pictures to make inferences. Circle the <u>best</u> answers.

Picture 1

You are walking past a church and see rose petals littering the sidewalk out front. What kind of inferences can you make?

A. There was an accident, and someone dropped rose petals.
B. Some kids were pulling rose petals off roses.

C. It must be Valentine's Day!
D. Flower girls dropped some rose petals from a wedding.

Picture 2

You see a fisherman fishing by himself on a beach or seashore. What can you infer?

A. The fisherman must be lost.
B. The fisherman is waiting for the tide to come in.

C. The fisherman does not want to be there.
D. The fisherman is comfortable and accustomed to fishing alone.

Picture 3

You see a shark getting close to a boy in the water, and the boy continues playing. What can you infer?

A. The boy did not see the shark.
B. The shark is not aiming to attack the boy.

C. The boy knew the shark could not see him.
D. The shark is attacking the boy.

Picture 4

You are walking through a wooded area, and you see a scared cat hiding in a tree. What can you infer?

A. The cat is hunting.
B. A dog chased the cat into the woods.

C. The cat enjoys hiding in trees.
D. Nobody wants the cat.

C. You can make inferences based on texts.
Example 1

Read the sentences.

A poor lost dog followed Harry and his little sister home from school, and tried to come into the house. They shut the door. When they opened it again, the dog was still there. He looked so sad. The children felt sorry for him.

Various. *Chambers's Elementary Science Readers* / Book I (Kindle Locations 930).

Question: What would the kids do?

1. Use prior knowledge.

   I had a dog as a pet, and I loved him very much. I have seen lost dogs, and I felt sad for them.

2. Use text clues.

   The dog tried to follow them into the house. When they opened the door, the dog was still there. The kids felt sorry for the dog.

3. Be a reading detective.

   If I were Harry or his sister, what would I do? I would ask my mom if I could keep the dog.

4. Make an inference.

   I think the children would ask their mom if they could keep the dog.

Make an inference.

An inference is an educated guess. You **view the situation** or read the text, you **think of prior knowledge** of the situation or context, and you **make an educated guess**. It is that simple!

Example 2

   Read the passage. **Make an inference.**

The cat knew that he would not hurt her, so she kept her claws in, and let him feel them on the outside. **First of all**, he found under the paw a soft, smooth pad.

"Now I know how it is that she can walk so softly!" he said. "This must help her to walk in that way."

Now pussy gave a great yawn, and stretched out her paws, claws and all. Harry saw the sharp nails like hooks.

Various. *Chambers's Elementary Science Readers / Book I* (Kindle Locations 919-924).

Question: Would the cat scratch Harry?

1. Use prior knowledge.

Cats can scratch you if they are angry with you. They can also scratch you if they do not like you.

2. Use text clues.

The text says the cat knew he would not hurt her, so I do not think she would hurt him.

3. Be a reading detective.

The cat yawned, so she was happy and maybe sleepy. She stretched out her claws and paws. Harry saw the sharp claws, but I do not think he was afraid.

4. Make an inference.

The cat would not hurt Harry.

Exercise 3
Use your prior knowledge to make inferences about the pictures below.

Picture 1

Picture 2

REFLECTION ON LEARNING

Answer the following reflection questions, and feel free to discuss your responses with your teacher or classmate.

- What reading idea or strategy did you learn from this section?

- What new concepts did you learn?

- What methods did you work on in this section?

- What aspect of this section is still not 100 percent clear for you?

- What do you want your teacher to know?

LESSON 6

USING VISUAL IMAGERY

By the end of this lesson, you will learn to use visual imagery to understand text and make meaning.

Visual imagery involves making pictures in your head as you read. As we said earlier, readers use prior knowledge and experience to find meaning in a text. Visual imagery will also help you experience the reading in greater detail and remember what you read.

Look at the picture of the man and the woman.

Where are they? What are they doing? What are they thinking? Why is he smiling?

Use your senses when you make images in your head. Ask yourself these questions: What do I hear when I read the text? What do I see? What can I touch? What can I taste? What can I smell?

Visual imagery will help you remember what you read when you are reading the following:

A Description

Imagery can be used with any descriptive passage. You can visualize scenes, people and places.

A Narrative

When you read a story, you can picture the story's setting. You can also imagine the characters or people in the reading.

Always note the **"evidence"** or the words in the passage that help you create your mental picture.

You can also **draw a picture of what you see in your head**, using words and phrases from the text to support your reasoning.

Example 1

Read the short passage below.

"Take that!" cried Andy, raising his whip, with the intention of slashing Tom across the face, for the front of the auto was open.

But the blow never fell, for, the next instant, the carriage gave a lurch as one of the wheels slid against a stone, and, as Andy was standing up, and leaning forward, he was pitched head first out into the road.

What can you see? Can you see the raised whip?   Can you see the car move forward?   What can you hear? Can you hear Andy speak?   Can you hear the anger in his voice?   What can you see? Can you see Andy leaning forward before the auto hit him? Can you see the front of the auto open?   Can you see Andy pitching forward?   Can you see Andy lying on the road?

Remember: Making pictures in your head as you read will help you

Example 2

Can you use prior knowledge, inferences and visual imagery to understand what is happening in the picture below?

Exercise 1
Read the questions and <u>circle</u> the letter for the best answer.

1. Are the people indoors or outdoors?`

   A. They are indoors.   B. They are outdoors.

2. What made you choose indoors or outdoors?

   A. I can see a kitchen.   B. People usually grill outside.

3. What kind of event or party do you think it is?

   A. It is a Christmas celebration.
   B. It is a Thanksgiving Day picnic.

   C. It is a 4th of July event.
   D. It is a Halloween event.

4. How do you know? Write your answer below.

_____

Exercise 2

Can you use prior knowledge, inferences and visual imagery to understand what is happening in the picture below?

What is happening in this picture? Choose the <u>best</u> answer from the choices.

1. What is the occasion?

A. The man's wedding
B. A nature walk

C. A graduation
D. Dropping out of school

2. Which of the following best supports your answer to Part A?

A. He is smiling, and he has on a tuxedo.
B. He is wearing a graduation gown and holding his cap.

C. He is wearing hiking gear.
D. He is laughing.

REFLECTION ON LEARNING

Answer the following reflection questions, and feel free to discuss your responses with your teacher or classmate.

- What reading idea or strategy did you learn from this section?

- What new concepts did you learn?

- What methods did you work on in this section?

- What aspect of this section is still not 100 percent clear for you?

- What do you want your teacher to know?

LESSON 7

BUILDING VOCABULARY AND USING CONTEXT CLUES

What does the word mean in the context?

Find clues.

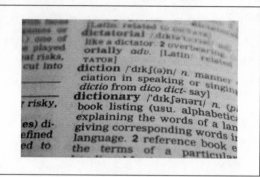

By the end of this lesson, you will have increased your knowledge of using context clues to unlock the meaning of unknown words.

When you read a passage, there may be words you do not know. However, the writer puts **clues** (words, phrases and sentences) near the unknown words to help you figure out the meanings of the words as you read.

Some types of clues are synonyms, antonyms, definitions or explanations and examples. You can use the context to infer or guess the meaning of each word based on what is going on in the reading.

Synonym or Restatement Clues

Synonyms are words that have the same or similar meanings. In using a synonym or restatement clue, the author says the same thing twice but in different ways. The signal word "**or**" may be used.

In a synonym clue, the author says the same thing twice in different ways.

Examine the following examples.

1. "When you look at the image, you need to interpret it by questioning what it connotes **or** suggests."

The writer uses the word "connotes" and then explains that the meaning of the word is "suggests."

2. "Her rancor **or** hatred for meeting new people resulted in her living a life of loneliness."

The writer used the word "rancor" and the synonym "hatred" immediately after. So, we know that "rancor" means "hatred."

Antonym or Contrast Clues

Antonyms are words opposite in meaning. The writer tells you what the word does not mean. Often the signal words "**but**," "**although**" and "**however**" are used to signal that an opposite thought is coming up.

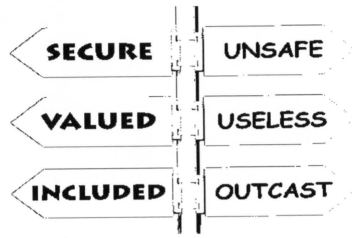

Examine the following examples.

3. "I <u>abhor</u> spending hours shopping for clothes, **but** I <u>adore</u> shopping for groceries."

Based on the context, the reader knows that to "abhor" something is to dislike it very much, but to "adore" something is to love it very much.

4. "When the light is bright, the pupils of the eyes <u>contract;</u> **however**, the pupils <u>dilate</u> in darkness."

Based on the context, the reader knows the opposite of the word "contract" is "dilate." To "contract" means to get smaller and to "dilate" means to get bigger.

Definition or Explanation Clues

Using this type of context clue, the writer defines the word for you in the form of an explanation. Clues to identifying a definition include "**that is**" and the use of commas, dashes and parentheses.

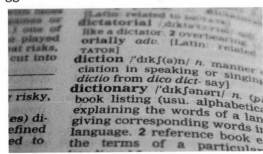

Exercise 1
Examine the following sentences and answer the questions that follow.

1. Her **emaciation**, that is, her skeleton-like appearance, was very alarming and scary.

What is the <u>best</u> meaning of *emaciation* as used in the sentence?

A. Slim
B. Obese or fat
C. Like a skeleton
D. Muscular

2. **Sedentary** individuals—people who are not very active—often suffer from poor health and chronic diseases.

What is the <u>best</u> meaning of *sedentary* as used in the sentence?

A. Inactive
B. Active
C. Moving slowly
D. Moving

Example Clues

With this clue, the writer will place an example near the unknown word to explain the meaning. Often the writer uses signals words like "**such as**," "**for example**" and "**including**."

Exercise 2
Examine the following sentences and answer the questions that follow.

1. **Celestial** bodies, including the stars, the moon and the sun, have fascinated humans for ages.

What is the <u>best</u> meaning of *celestial* as used in the sentence?

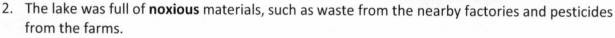

A. Heavenly bodies
B. Relating to outer space
C. Bright
D. Nightly

2. The lake was full of **noxious** materials, such as waste from the nearby factories and pesticides from the farms.

What is the <u>best</u> meaning of *noxious* as used in the sentence?

A. Very harmful
B. Harmless
C. Unpleasant
D. Beneficial

NOTE: When you are able, always consult a dictionary.

REFLECTION ON LEARNING

Answer the following reflection questions, and feel free to discuss your responses with your teacher or classmate.

- What reading idea or strategy did you learn from this section?

- What new concepts did you learn?

- What methods did you work on in this section?

- What aspect of this section is still not 100 percent clear for you?

- What do you want your teacher to know?

LESSON 8

UNDERSTANDING QUESTION-ANSWER RELATIONSHIPS

By the end of this lesson, you will learn more about self-questioning and question-answer relationships.

Self-questioning is a reading strategy that keeps your mind active and alert as you read. To understand what you read, you need to ask questions about the text. Ask questions **BEFORE** you read, **DURING** your reading of the text and **AFTER** reading.

Before Reading	During Reading	After Reading
What do I know about this topic?	What do I want to know about this topic?	What new information have I learned about this topic?

Question-answer relationships (QARs) will make you aware of the different types of questioning you need to use when reading a text.

To begin, you always need to **ask questions of the text** before you read and as you read. We have already discussed one type of self-questioning: asking previewing or pre-reading questions when you activate your background knowledge.

BEFORE you read: Study **titles** and **pictures** before reading to activate your prior knowledge. Also, use self-questioning to preview the text before you read. Make predictions and then read to see if your predictions are correct. Ask yourself, "What do I know about this topic?"

You can also read the **first sentence** and any **boldfaced** or *italicized* words. Ask yourself, "Why has the writer highlighted this word? What does the word mean?"

DURING reading: You need to think about what you are thinking. When you are asking yourself questions and answering the questions based on the text, you need to determine whether the questions are **literal questions**, **inference questions** or **evaluative questions**.

There are three types of questions:

1) **Literal Questions:** The answer to a literal question is **right there** in the text.

	Answers to literal questions are **RIGHT THERE** in the text.

2) **Inference Questions:** To answer inference questions, you need to think deeply, use context clues and go beyond what is stated in the text. These are sometimes called **"think and search"** questions because you have to figure out the answers.

To answer
inference questions,
you must
THINK AND SEARCH.

3) **Evaluative Questions:** To answer evaluative questions, you need to examine different viewpoints, make a judgment and take a position. These are often called **"on my own"** questions.

Is it half full or half empty?
With evaluative questions, you must
TAKE A POSITION.

Practice Exercise

Examine the picture below. Can you formulate and answer the literal, inferential and evaluative questions about the picture?

LITERAL – The answers are right there.

1. What is happening?	Some people are bathing a dog.
2. What color is the dog?	The dog is black.
3. Where is the dog?	The dog is in a tub.
4. How many people are in the picture?	_____

INFERENTIAL – Think deeply and use clues from the picture.

1. Is the dog happy?	_____
2. How can you tell?	_____
3. Does the dog like to be bathed?	_____
4. Why do you think so many people are washing the dog?	_____

EVALUATIVE – You are on your own. Use your experience, background and the picture to answer the questions.

1. What could the people have done to make the dog more comfortable?	_____
2. Do you think this dog is bathed often? Why or why not?	_____
3. If you had a dog, how often would you bathe him or her?	_____

AFTER reading: After you have completed a reading, you may be asked to answer post-reading questions. These are designed to assess what you have learned about the topic or reading.

REFLECTION ON LEARNING

Answer the following reflection questions, and feel free to discuss your responses with your teacher or classmate.

- What reading idea or strategy did you learn from this section?

- What new concepts did you learn?

- What methods did you work on in this section?

- What aspect of this section is still not 100 percent clear for you?

- What do you want your teacher to know?

LESSON 9
LEARNING NON-FICTION TEXT FEATURES

Fiction Texts or Stories

When most readers begin reading, they read stories or narratives, and poems and rhymes.

Non-Fiction Texts

As you mature as a reader, you will need to read non-fiction texts.

In the higher grades in school, the focus on reading changes to non-fiction books. **How do non-fiction books differ from fiction books?**

Non-fiction texts contain true or factual information. These texts include science, social studies, mathematics and history books. These texts have a great deal of information that students need to learn.

> **Non-fiction books contain factual information.**

Text Features

Text features include the table of contents, index, glossary, headings, captions, graphs, charts and so on. There is a great number of non-fiction text features, and you will learn about them in this section.

Why are text features important to the reader?

Text features highlight important information for the reader. You can use the **table of contents** and the **index** to quickly identify the subject or topic area you want to read about. If you are researching, these features can help you quickly know whether the book has the information you need. Without the table of contents and the index, you will waste time flipping through a book to search for the information you need.

Furthermore, special print types like **boldface** and *italics* make useful information jump out and grab your attention.

Now, let's examine a non-fiction book titled ***Planet Earth***: *More than 100 Questions and Answers to Things You Want to Know*. The author is Ian James.

A. **The Table of Contents** – The table of contents page is a list of the topics discussed in the book.

B. **The Index** – The index is an alphabetic listing at the back of the text. The information is provided in names, phrases or single words, and it tells you on what pages you can find the specific information in the book.

Example:

Index

AB	NO
Atlantic Ocean 7, 30	Ocean ridges and trenches
C	6-7, 8, 10
Carbon 13, 14	**WXYZ**
DEF	Wegener, Alfred 6
Earthquakes 7, 8-9	Yellowstone National Park 27

C. **Glossary**

The glossary is like a small dictionary that is related to the book. It defines new words contained in the book and lists the words in alphabetical order. It is found at the back of the book.

Glossary

Explosive volcanoes – Explosive eruptions occur when the magma is thick and contains explosive gas. **Springs** – Springs occur when ground water flows on the surface.	**Tributary rivers** – Tributaries are rivers that flow into a main river. **Trace fossil** – Trace fossils give information about animals that lived in ancient times.

D. **Special Print** – Bold Print, Italics or Underlined Words

Writers of non-fiction texts use bold print, italics and underlining to highlight important words. Your eyes will be drawn to these words, which are important for you to note.

Question 1: In which of the following books are you most likely to find a glossary?

A. A fairy tale

B. A history book

C. A book of poems

D. A crossword book

Question 2: Where would you find the glossary in a non-fiction book?

A. At the front of the book

B. At the center of the book

C. At the end of the book

D. Nowhere in the book

Non-Fiction Text Features Chart

Name of Text Feature	Purpose	Example
Title Page	The title page has the title of the book, the name of the author, and sometimes, the name of the illustrator.	***Planet Earth*** *More than 100 Questions and Answers to Things You Want to Know*
Table of Contents	The Table of Contents is located at the front of the book. Sometimes, it is only called "**CONTENTS.**" It shows the **titles** of the **chapters** and the pages where the chapters are located.	**Contents** Earth History ....4 The Changing Earth ....6 Earthquakes .... 8 Shaping the Land ....16 Deserts ....22 Facts and Figures .... 30 Index......................................32 Glossary 34
Index	The index is an *alphabetic list* at the back of the book. It shows you where to find specific information in the text on a topic, word or person.	Example: Europe 7, 20, 21, 22, 24, 25 Earthquakes 7, 8-10
Glossary	This is similar to a dictionary. The glossary identifies specific vocabulary related to the topic and defines them.	**The Amazon** – The Amazon drains a huge region that contains the world's largest rainforest. **Fossils** – the preserved remains or impression of a prehistoric creature or thing

Headings and Subheadings	Headings and subheadings help the reader identify the main ideas and how sub-ideas relate to the main idea.	Headings are in large print at the top of the page and the beginning of the reading. Subheadings appear in the reading in smaller print. For example:
		
		 VOLCANO ERUPTIONS
		     Dormant Volcano
		     Extinct volcano
		     Explosive volcano

Captions	These are very brief and could be a short phrase or one or two short sentences placed near a picture or another type of graphic to help the reader understand the picture.	**Fossil animal biology**

Special Print • Bold print • *Italics* • <u>Underlined</u>	When a word or phrase is in **bold print**, *italics,* or <u>underlined</u>, the writer wants the reader to know it is important.	The Dutch created new land by building **dikes** (sea walls) around areas once under the sea, called *polders*.
Charts and Graphs	Charts and graphs show data related to the topic or information in the text.	 Writers may use bar graphs, pie charts or plot lines.
Photos	Photos can show you a near view or a far view. If the text is discussing the Grand Canyon, for example, there may be several pictures from different angles.	The Grand Canyon – Winter View
Timelines	Timelines give the order of events. They are often used in history to show the time span over which changes took place. The example here shows how fashion has changed.	
Labeled Diagrams	These show detailed parts of an object, animal or plant, so the reader can see and learn about the various parts.	

Sidebars/Text Box	Sidebars are set apart from the main text on the side or bottom of a page. They give more information about a detail in the text.	The butterflies lay their eggs. From these hatch worms or caterpillars, which change their skins several times to become **chrysalides** or silkworms, out of which come the beautiful butterflies. ───────── **chrysalides** – the hard, outer cases enclosing dormant insect pupae, especially butterflies or moths
Maps	Maps help readers see the location where information in the text comes from or the place the author is discussing. Example: The Amazon River in South America contains far more water than any other river. (The author provides a map of South America.)	

Practice Tasks

Creating a Text-Feature Booklet

   Examine several non-fiction books. Create a booklet that features the different text features introduced in this lesson.

Using Search Tools

   Sometimes, you will need to conduct online research on a topic. Conduct a keyword search using online search tools. Let's say you need to research the **type of music** popular with people under the age of twenty-five. Begin by coming up with a **keyword or key phrase** to type into Google or another search engine.

   You can search for "types of music," but this will give you a lot of information you do not need. You can search for "popular music," but again, this might give you too much unnecessary information. Instead, you can use "and" to join phrases, for example, "popular music and youth." You can also use quotation marks to narrow your search further. Quotation marks make the search engine search for that exact phrase, for example, "music popular with youth."

Using Icons

An icon is a picture displayed on a computer screen that you can click on. The purpose of the icon is to help computer users move quickly to different locations on the computer. When the user double-clicks on the icon, it opens. Two popular icons are the Google and Safari search engine icons.

Other Popular Icons

W – Windows icon **X** – Excel icon **A** – App store icon	**F** – Facebook **T** – Twitter icon

Electronic Menus

The main purpose of an electronic menu is to help you find your way around a program or website and locate the information you need. It lets you know what choices are available for your use.

Creating Hyperlinks

A hyperlink is a link on the web to another resource on the web. It could be a reference to data, a picture, webpage, website or file. When you click on the hyperlink, it takes you to that data, picture, webpage, website or different document. Hyperlinks are underlined and usually in color, often blue. When your mouse pointer changes to a pointing finger, you are hovering over a hyperlink.

When you conduct Google searches, every search result you get is a hyperlink to a different website.

How to Create Hyperlinks

Do the following to create a hyperlink:

1. Save the document you want to insert the hyperlink into.
2. Select the text or picture you want to add as a hyperlink. You can link to a webpage, a document or an e-mail.
3. On the Insert tab in Word, click "Hyperlink."
4. When the hyperlink opens, in the "Link to" box, enter the address or the URL of the webpage that you want to link to. If the document is on your desktop when you click "Select," the browser will go to your desktop where the address is located.
5. Click "Select."

REFLECTION ON LEARNING

Answer the following reflection questions, and feel free to discuss your responses with your teacher or classmate.

- What reading idea or strategy did you learn from this section?

- What new concepts did you learn?

- What methods did you work on in this section?

- What aspect of this section is still not 100 percent clear for you?

- What do you want your teacher to know?

LESSON 10
READING FOR MAIN IDEAS

In this lesson, you will learn how to identify the topic and the main idea of a reading.

Example 1

Scorpions

This is one of the largest of the insect tribe. Scorpions in <u>different countries</u> are of various <u>sizes</u>, from two or three inches to nearly a foot in length. It somewhat resembles a lobster, and casts its skin, as the lobster does its shell. Scorpions are common in hot <u>countries</u>. They are very bold and watchful. When anything approaches, they erect their tails, and stand ready to inflict the direful sting.

In some parts of <u>Italy and France</u>, they are among the greatest pests that plague mankind. They are very <u>numerous</u>, and are most <u>common</u> in old houses, in dry or decayed walls, and among furniture, insomuch that it is attended, with much danger to remove the same. Their sting is generally a very deadly poison, though not in all cases, owing to a difference of **malignity** of different animals, or some other cause.

Unknown. *The History of Insects* (Kindle Locations 95-97).

How to Find the Precise Topic

To begin, find **the precise topic**. The general topic is given in many paragraphs but not the precise topic. The general topic is usually very broad. The precise topic is more limited.

The topic of the above passage is "scorpions." But this topic seems to be very general or broad. To find the precise topic, look for repeated words or phrases. As you examine the text, you can underline or highlight the <u>repeated words</u> or phrases. The repeated words or phrases can point you towards the specific or precise topic. The precise topic is "<u>scorpions in different countries</u>."

How to Find the Main Idea

To find the main idea, ask yourself, "What does the writer want to say about the topic?" Often, writers state the main idea in a topic sentence at the beginning or very early in the paragraph. We can find the main idea in this text in the second sentence.

Main Idea:

Scorpions in different countries are of various sizes, from two or three inches to nearly a foot in length.

How to Find Supporting Sentences

Supporting sentences develop and expand the main idea. These sentences tell you more about the main idea. Some are called **major supporting** sentences, and others are **minor supporting** sentences. The major supporting sentences tell you more about the main idea sentence. The minor supporting sentences give you more details or explanations about the major sentences.

Topic
Scorpions in different countries

Main idea
Scorpions in different countries are two or three inches to nearly a foot in length.

Major Supporting Details	**Minor Supporting Details**
1. Scorpions are similar to lobsters . . .	1. They are bold and watchful.
2. Scorpions are common in hot countries.	2. When anyone approaches, they. . .
3. In Italy and France, they are great pests.	3. They are numerous and common in old houses.
4. Their sting could be deadly.	

A Word about Prefixes

A **prefix** is a letter (or a group of letters) placed at the beginning of a word to change the meaning of the word. For example, the prefix "un-" is placed before the word "happy" to create the word "unhappy." The prefix "un" means "not."

The prefix "**mal**" means bad. So you can guess that the word **malignity** means something bad.

The following sentence tells us that the scorpion's sting is usually poisonous. However, not in every case; different scorpions' stings have different effects.

Their sting is generally a very deadly poison, though not in all cases, owing to a difference of **malignity** of different animals, or some other cause.

The word *malignity* means danger or harmfulness.

Example 2

Geese Hunting

Smith and I were about a hundred yards from them [the flock of Canada geese], when Murphy scared them. They rose in a **dense** mass and came directly between Smith and me. We were about gunshot distance apart, and they were not over thirty feet in the air.

We opened up on them with our pump guns and No. 5 shot. When the smoke cleared away and we had rounded up the **cripples** we found, we had twenty-one geese. I have heard of bigger killings out in this country, but never **positively** knew of them.

William T. Hornaday. *Our Vanishing Wild Life: Its Extermination and Preservation* (Kindle Locations 3711-3714).

Words and Their Meanings Based on the Text

Dense	Very thick, a great number
Cripples	Having difficulty walking, lame
Positively	Sure, certain

A. **Find the precise topic**.

In many paragraphs, the general topic is given but not the precise topic. Remember, the general topic is usually very broad. The precise topic is more limited. If we look at the passage, the title seems to fit the reading. The passage describes "Geese Hunting."

Topic: Geese hunting

B. **Next, find the main idea.**

How do you find the main idea? To find the main idea, ask yourself, "What does the writer want to say about geese hunting?"

Question 1: Which of the following is the best main idea of the passage?

    A. The hunters shot some geese.
    B. The geese were flying in a dense mass.
    C. The hunters shot twenty-one birds, and this was their biggest goose-killing.
    D. The hunters loved to shoot birds.

C. Find the major supporting details.

Major supporting sentences give you more details about the main idea.

Question 2: Which of the following is a major supporting sentence?

    A. The smoke cleared away.
    B. We found we had twenty-one geese.
    C. Both shot at the geese.
    D. Smith and I were about a hundred yards from them.

Evaluative Question: Do you support the hunting of wild birds or wild animals? Why or why not?

_____

_____

_____

REFLECTION ON LEARNING

Answer the following reflection questions, and feel free to discuss your responses with your teacher or classmate.

- What reading idea or strategy did you learn from this section?

- What new concepts did you learn?

- What methods did you work on in this section?

- What aspect of this section is still not 100 percent clear for you?

- What do you want your teacher to know?

LESSON 11
UNDERSTANDING WHAT YOU READ

By the end of this lesson, you will learn how to monitor your comprehension and use fix-up strategies when comprehension is lacking.

Often when you are reading, your comprehension breaks down and you realize you are not understanding the text. When you realize you are not getting the meaning or do not understand, you need to take certain steps to improve your comprehension. This procedure or act of taking steps **"to fix up" gaps in comprehension** is called **comprehension monitoring**.

When you monitor your comprehension, you will know when you understand what you read and when you do not. To monitor your comprehension, do the following:

- As you read, be aware of what you do not understand.
- When you don't understand, admit to yourself, "I don't understand what I am reading."
- Identify exactly what it is you do not understand.
- Use appropriate strategies to resolve the problems in understanding.

You Read a Passage, but You Don't Understand

STOP and ask:	Why doesn't this make sense? Why don't I understand what I am reading?
THINK and ask:	Where did I lose track? Do I not know the meaning of a word? Did my mind wander? Do I not know enough about the topic? Can I state the main point of the reading? Is the meaning in the text or in my head?

REACT – Take Action to Help You Understand

I don't know the meaning of a word. What do I do?	I can use context clues to figure out the meaning. I can use a dictionary. I can slow down my reading. I can reread sections of the text.

I don't understand what I am reading. What can I do?	I can read ahead and, maybe the meaning will become clear. I can identify the topic and activate my background knowledge.

The material is difficult to understand. What can I do?	I can try to create a visual image of the material. I can make meaning from the headings and pictures.

REFLECTION ON LEARNING

Answer the following reflection questions, and feel free to discuss your responses with your teacher or classmate.

- What reading idea or strategy did you learn from this section?

- What new concepts did you learn?

- What methods did you work on in this section?

- What aspect of this section is still not 100 percent clear for you?

- What do you want your teacher to know?

LESSON 12
USING TEXT STRUCTURE TO BUILD READING COMPREHENSION

By the end of this lesson, you will be able to read, understand and describe the structures of texts that address **time order**, **sequencing** and **cause and effect**.

What Is Text Structure?

Writers use patterns when they write. When you read a text, it helps you to understand the meaning if you identify the pattern. There are several types of text structures, but we will only look at three of them in this manual.

A. **Time-Order Text Structure**

In **time-order structures**, actions and events are presented as they occur in time. This pattern is used for stories or narratives because narratives proceed in the order in which the events happen.

Some of the **transitions,** or signal words, that writers use to signal time order are given below:

• First	• Now
• Second	• Before
• Third	• Sometimes
• Next	• Never
• After, after this	• Last, lastly, finally
• Suddenly	• Then, therefore
• When, while	• Soon
• After, afterwards	• Suddenly
• Today, tomorrow, yesterday	• Meanwhile

Exercise 1

Read the passage. As you read, try to **visualize** the scene.

The Grey Wolf

Before us, in plain view was a great **rabble** of Dogs. Some were large and small, black, white, and yellow. They were wriggling and heaving this way and that way in a rude ring. Next, there was a little yellow Dog stretched and quiet in the snow. Meanwhile, on the outer part of the ring was a huge black Dog. He was jumping about and barking, but keeping behind the moving mob.

Then in the midst, the center and cause of it all, was a great, grim, Wolf. Wolf? He looked like a Lion. There he stood, all alone—calm—with **bristling** mane, and legs braced firmly. Now, he was glancing this way and that, to be ready for an attack in any direction. There was a curl on his lips. It looked like scorn, but I suppose it was really the fighting snarl of tooth display.

Led by a wolfish-looking Dog that should have been ashamed, the pack suddenly dashed in. The great gray wolf leaped here and there. As he attacked, chop, chop, chop went those fearful jaws. Then there was a death yelp from more than one of his **foes**. Afterwards, those that were able again sprang back. He stood before them fearless.

I wished the train would stick in a snowdrift, as it did so often before. For all my heart went out to that Gray—wolf! I longed to go and help him. But the snow-deep **glade** flashed by, the tree trunks shut out the view, and soon, we went on to our journey's end.

_____
Ernest Thompson Seton. *Animal Heroes* (Kindle Locations 1705-1711).

Vocabulary

<u>Rabble</u> of dogs	A disorderly pack
<u>Bristling</u> mane	Stiff and spiky hair
One of his <u>foes</u>	Enemies
The snow deep <u>glade</u> flashed by	An open space in a forest

Question 1: In the passage, underline and then list at least four transitions that signal time-order.

_____

_____

_____

_____

Question 2: What happened? List the **correct order** in which the events happened.

1	What happened first?	A. Removed from the ring was a huge, barking black dog.
2	What happened second?	B. The grey wolf attacked and injured several dogs.
3	What followed?	C. In the center was a great wolf warrior.
4	What happened next?	D. The pack dashed in.
5	What happened next?	E. The traveler saw a pack of rowdy dogs in a ring.
6	What happened last?	F. The train went by the scene.

Question 3: Which of these <u>best</u> states the topic for the reading?

A. The Winnipeg Wolf

B. The Wolfish-Looking Dog

C. The Grey Wolf Warrior

D. The Lion-Looking Wolf

Questions 4:

Part A

Which sentence <u>best</u> states the main idea of the reading?

A. The grey wolf was a wolfish-looking dog.

B. The writer's heart went out to that grey wolf.

C. The grey wolf fought the other dogs alone.

D. The grey wolf was a lonely, untamed warrior who faced his enemies fearlessly.

Part B

Which two sentences support the answer to Part A?

A. The pack suddenly dashed in.

B. As he attacked, chop, chop, chop went his fearless jaws.

C. A huge black dog was jumping and barking.

D. There was a curl on his lips.

E. He stood before them fearless.

Exercise 2

Here is another example of a <u>time-order text structure</u>.

In addition to narratives or stories, time order is also used in science and history.

The Butterfly

There are many kinds of butterflies. This wonderful class of insects goes through many changes. First, the butterflies lay their eggs. Next, these hatch out worms or caterpillars, which change their skins several times. Finally, they become chrysalis, or silkworms, out of which come the beautiful butterflies.

Unknown. *The History of Insects* (Kindle Locations 123-125).

Question 1: How many stages does the butterfly go through?

Question 2: What happens? List the stages in order:

What happened first?	
What happened next?	
What happened next?	
What happened last?	

Question 3: Write three time-order signal words from the passage.

1. _____

2. _____

3. _____

B. Sequence Text Structure

What is sequencing?

Sequencing is the order in which things happen. It could be **steps in a story** or **process**. For example, what happens first, next and last.

Clue words such as *first, next* and *before* tell you when something happens. Your car manual is written in a sequence format. Your TV manual and cookbooks are also written in sequence format. If you were reading a passage on "How to make pizza," or "How to vacuum your carpet," the sequence pattern would be used.

Parents use sequencing.

You learned sequencing as a child, and if you are a parent, you certainly use sequencing in helping your children be disciplined and learn to organize their lives. Most parents have an evening schedule their children are to follow that may go like this: first, you will eat dinner and then have a bath and read a story before you go to bed.

Example 1

Use visual imagery. Make pictures in your mind as you follow the **sequence** in the following process:

How to make a bowl of vegetable soup!

Sequence – Steps in a Process

First – Get everything you need.	**Second – Clean, cut and begin cooking.**
Third – Stir the pot and cook well.	**Fourth – Enjoy!**

Below are some transitions used in sequences:

• 1, 2, 3, 4, 5	• Following this
• First, second, third	• At this time, At this point
• First of all	• Now
• To begin with	• Previously, Before this
• Next	• After, Afterward
• Then	• Subsequently
• Finally, At last	• Meanwhile

Example 2

Read the following passage.

The Cat

The cat knew that he would not hurt her, so she kept her claws in, and let him feel them on the outside. **First of all**, he found under the paw a soft smooth pad.

"Now I know how it is that she can walk so softly!" he said. "This must help her to walk in that way."

Now pussy gave a great yawn, and stretched out her paws, claws and all. Harry saw the sharp nails like hooks, and watched them go back into their sheaths. **Then** she curled herself up on his lap. **Afterwards**, he took hold of one of her hind-feet, and found only four toes upon it.

_____

Various. *Chambers's Elementary Science Readers* / Book I (Kindle Locations 919-924).

Exercise 3
Read the story events below.

Story Events
- A. He found a smooth, soft pad under the paw.
- B. The cat kept in her claws.
- C. Harry saw the sharp nails like hooks.
- D. The cat gave a great yawn and stretched her paws.
- E. He looked at her hind feet and found only four toes.
- F. The cat curled up on his lap.

The story events are not in order. **Sequence the story** in the order the events happened. The first one is done for you.

B. The cat kept her claws in.

C. Cause-and-Effect Text Structures

A **cause** is why something happened. An **effect** is what happened.

Exercise 4

Effect: What happened?

There were several effects.
1. Houses broke apart.
2. Rubble was everywhere.
3. People were homeless.
4. Cars were smashed.
5. Streets were flooded.

Add two more effects:

6. _____

7. _____

What was the cause? It was an earthquake.

Exercise 5

There can be several causes and one effect.

Effect: Weight Loss

Causes

What caused the weight loss? List the four causes.

Exercise 6

The Race

At the halfway point, the pair were running neck and neck. Then the Pony slipped on the ice, and because he was afraid, he did not run as fast. The Colt bolted away. The Pony and his driver were far behind when a roar from every human throat in the stands told that the Colt had passed the wire and won the race.

Ernest Thompson Seton. *Animal Heroes* (Kindle Locations 2037-2040).

Question 1: The Colt won the race because

A. He was faster than the Pony.
B. The Pony slipped on the ice and did not run fast.

C. The Colt bolted away.
D. The Pony stopped running.

Vocabulary

Question 2: What does the word *bolted* mean?

A. To move very fast
B. To move slowly

C. To crawl
D. To run

Question 3: What word does <u>not</u> rhyme with *roar*?

A. Set

B. Boar

C. Soar

D. Door

REFLECTION ON LEARNING

Answer the following reflection questions, and feel free to discuss your responses with your teacher or classmate.

- What reading idea or strategy did you learn from this section?

- What new concepts did you learn?

- What methods did you work on in this section?

- What aspect of this section is still not 100 percent clear for you?

- What do you want your teacher to know?

LESSON 13

UNDERSTANDING POINT OF VIEW

Who is telling the story?
The point of view is the angle from which a story is told.

First Person - The narrator is telling the events from
his or her perspective.

1st Person Point of View	Examples	Look for These Pronouns
The first-person narrator tells the story by describing his or her thoughts and feelings.	**I** went to the store. Give it to **me.** **We** went to the store. **We** were all homeschooled.	*I, me, myself, me, mine, we*

Second Person - The writer speaks for you in the story.

2nd Person Point of View	Example	Look for These Pronouns
This point of view is used in letters, speeches and some stories.	"Oh, the places **you'**ll go!"- Dr. Seuss	*You, your, yours*

Third Person - The writer is an onlooker watching the action and describes the characters' thoughts, feelings and actions.

3rd Person Point of View	Example	Look for These Pronouns
The writer describes how other characters think and feel. **Limited –** Knowing one character's thoughts **Omniscient –** Knowing all the characters' thoughts	Sometimes **she** did not know what **she** wanted. If **she** feared the past or the future, **she** did not know.	*he, she, it, they, him, her*

The cat knew that he would not hurt her, so she kept her claws in, and let him feel them on the outside. **First of all**, he found under the paw a soft smooth pad. "Now I know how it is that she can walk so softly!" <u>he said</u>. "This must help her to walk in that way." _____ Various. *Chambers's Elementary Science Readers /* Book I (Kindle Locations 919-924).	**Question 1:** Look for clues. Who is talking? (*I, me, you, he, she, they*) What is the point of view? _____

Alice was beginning to get very tired of sitting by her sister on the bank, and of having nothing to do. Once or twice she had peeped into the book **her** sister was reading, but it had no pictures or conversations in it. _____ Lewis Carroll. *Alice's Adventures in Wonderland* (Kindle Locations 23-32).	**Question 2:** Look for clues. Who is talking? (*I, me, you, he, she, they*) What is the point of view? _____

Question 3: What is the point of view?

If ever I see / On bush or tree / Young birds in their pretty nest / I must not, in play / Steal the birds away / To grieve their mother's breast.

_____

James H. Fassett. *The Beacon Second Reader* (Kindle Locations 516-517).

     a. Write the clues: _____

     b. Who is talking? (*I, me, you, he, she, they*)

     c. What is the point of view? _____

Question 4: What is the point of view?

Where are you going, you little pig? "I'm leaving my mother, I'm growing so big." So big, young pig! So young, so big!

     a. Write the clues: _____

     b. Who is talking? (*I, me, you, he, she, they*)

     c. What is the point of view? _____

_____

     James H. Fassett. *The Beacon Second Reader* (Kindle Locations 792-793).

To find out if the narrator is using the third-person omniscient, ask yourself, "Does the narrator reveal the character's thoughts and feelings?"

Imagine you are hidden and watching the character's behavior.

If you can see it or hear it, then it is an action or behavior.	Can you **see** the actions? Can you **hear** what the character is saying? **Do you know what the character is feeling?**

REFLECTION ON LEARNING

Answer the following reflection questions, and feel free to discuss your responses with your teacher or classmate.

- What reading idea or strategy did you learn from this section?

- What new concepts did you learn?

- What methods did you work on in this section?

- What aspect of this section is still not 100 percent clear for you?

- What do you want your teacher to know?

LESSON 14

HOW TO READ MAPS, CHARTS AND DATA TABLES

Graphics are used to show information. This information can be in the form of some type of visual. Below are examples of data in a picture, pie chart and chart.

A. Writers sometimes show information in a picture.	B. Writers sometimes show information in a pie chart.	C. Writers sometimes show information in a bar chart.
	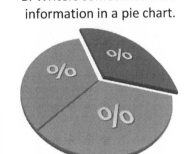	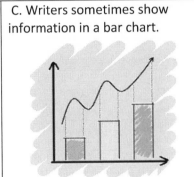

Pie charts and bar graphs are used often.

A. **Writers show information in pictures**.

This picture is in the form of a GPS map.

What does it show?

It shows major highways and directions to First Avenue.

When you see information in a picture, ask yourself, "What type of picture is this? What does the writer want me to see in this picture?"

B. **Writers show information in pie charts.**

Think of a pizza cut into slices.

Pie charts show different percentages (%) of data. Each slice shows a category. All portions add up to 100 percent.

Example: Below is an example of the information put into the pie chart shown above and how to read it.

Teaching Methods Teachers Use Most Often	
Whole-group instruction	40%
Small-group instruction	30%
Individual instruction	?

Question 1: What is the value of the missing percentage?

Write the missing percentage. Remember that the percentages must add up to 100.

C. Writers show information in bar charts or bar graphs.

Bar Graphs A graph compares data using bars of different lengths or heights to show values.	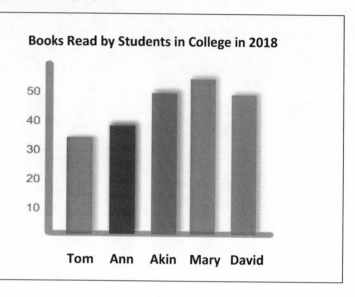

What is a bar graph or chart?

A bar graph compares data by using bars of different lengths or heights.

1) Look for the **title** of the chart.

The title: **Books Read by Students in College in 2018**

2) Look at the information on the side and the bottom.

At the bottom is the **horizontal axis**, also called the **x**-axis. In this diagram, there are **names** of five students.

3) The information on the side is on the **vertical axis.** This is also called the **y**-axis.

The vertical axis shows the quantity, with numbers from 10 to 50.

Based on the title, what do you think these numbers represent?

It shows the number of books read by each student in 2018.

4) **Why are bars in this bar graph of different heights?**

The bars are of different heights because the information is different for each person represented.

Who read the most books? _____
The chart shows that Mary read the most: more than 50 books.

Who read the fewest books? _____

84

That's right: Tom read the fewest books.

> So, you read a bar chart (graph) by studying the information on the horizontal and vertical axes.
> You then interpret what the information represents.

5) You also need to interpret **the scale.**

A scale is a set of numbers that represents the data organized in equal intervals.

In what pattern is the data organized above?

The data is organized in intervals of 10 (10, 20, 30, 40 and 50 books).

<u>**So, the scale is ten (10).**</u> Sometimes, a graph will give you a key that tells you the scale. The writer may place a number at the bottom of the horizontal axis in the left corner of the graph. The key and the scale are similar.

However, many writers do not give a key. Often **you have to figure out the key or scale.**

In this key or scale, the interval is 10. However, the intervals on a graph could be by fives, tens or even one-hundreds.

D. **Writers also use tables to organize information.**

Table: a way to organize and display data in rows and columns

Imagine you conducted a survey. You asked people what their favorite pizza is. You then organized the information in a table:

Most Popular Pizza	
Type of Pizza	**Number of Votes**
Pepperoni	30
Cheese	15
Hawaiian	6
Veggie	15
Chicken	9

Question 2: How many people provided answers to your survey? _____

How do you read a graph?

When you read a graph, you study or analyze the data on it. You are then able to interpret the data or explain what you learned.

6) **A Pie Chart of People's Favorite Pizzas**

We converted the votes on people's favorite pizza into a pie chart. We used percentages.

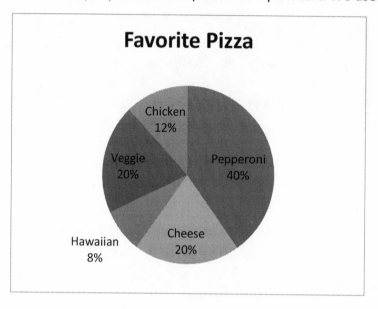

Question 3: How much do the totals add up to? _____

Practice Exercise
Examine the following chart and answer the questions that follow.

Reading a Bar Graph

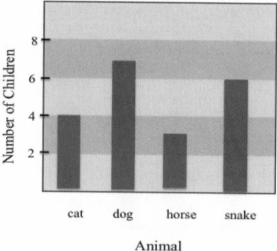

1. What is the title? _____

2. The graph is labeled on the side and at the bottom. <u>Labels</u> describe the information being shown.

    A. What label is on the horizontal (x) axis? _____

    B. What label is on the vertical (y) axis? _____

3. What is the <u>scale</u>? _____

4. Examine the data. Which animal was the favorite? _____

5. What animal was the least favorite? _____

REFLECTION ON LEARNING

Answer the following reflection questions, and feel free to discuss your responses with your teacher or classmate.

- What reading idea or strategy did you learn from this section?

- What new concepts did you learn?

- What methods did you work on in this section?

- What aspect of this section is still not 100 percent clear for you?

- What do you want your teacher to know?

LESSON 15
READING LONG PASSAGES

Passage 1
Read the passage and then answer the questions.

Needle-town

Harry and Dora once had a great treat. They went in the holidays to stay with an uncle and aunt who lived at a town where needles were made. We may call it Needle-town. While they were there, they were taken to the mills to see the needles made. The first room into which they went was very warm. It was called the wire-room.

A workman who was in the wire-room told them that it was filled with hot air night and day, so that no damp should come in and spoil the steel. All round the room, coils of steel-wire were hanging. They were wrapped up in paper, but the man took some of them down and let them look in. They saw that one coil was of very thick wire, while another was of wire as fine as a hair.

"One of these coils would be more than a mile long if it were stretched out straight," the man told Harry." Would you like to take hold of this one?" But

Harry found it too heavy, and it was hung up again on the wall. Then they went into another room, where a machine was cutting a coil of wire into bits.

"They are much too long for needles," said Dora, softly, to her uncle; but one of the **workmen** heard her, and said. "So they are! Each bit is going to be two needles. The two ends are to be the points, and the heads lie in the middle of the wire."

But no heads were to be seen yet. And the wire was not even straight, for it had long been rolled up in a coil. As the machine went on chopping, and the wire-strips dropped, a man picked them up and put them on a shelf in a sort of oven. There they were kept till they were red-hot, and then they were soft enough to be made straight.

Various. *Chambers's Elementary Science Readers* / Book I (Kindle Locations 730-746).

Questions 1 and 2:

1. Which word has a long /e/ vowel sound?
    A. heavy
    B. taken
    C. they
    D. treat
	2. How many syllables are in the word *workmen*?
	    A. 1
	    B. 2
	    C. 3
	    D. 4

Question 3: What is the precise topic of this passage?

A. A visit to Needle-town

B. Needles are made from wire strips

C. Harry and Dora once had a treat

D. How needles are made

Question 4:
Part A

Which sentence is the main idea of the article?

A. Needles are made through a long process.

B. To make needles, wire is cut into strips, placed into an oven, then straightened and cut into two.

C. The wire has to be very hot for the needles to be made.

D. Needle-making is an interesting process.

Part B
Which two sentences support the answer to Part A?

A. But no heads were to be seen yet.

B. Then they went into another room, where a machine was cutting a coil of wire into bits.

C. The first room was called the wire-room.

D. Each bit is going to be two needles.

E. They were kept in the oven till they were red-hot, and then they were soft enough to be made straight.

F. The first room into which they went was very warm.

Question 5: Which of the following is the text structure or the organizational pattern of the reading?

A. Compare and contrast

B. Sequence pattern

C. Time-order

D. Cause and effect

Question 6: Put the story in order of how the events happened. The first one is done for you.

A. The wire is picked up and placed into an oven until it is red hot.	A. Coils of wrapped wire are kept in a hot-air room.
B. When soft enough, the wire is straightened.	B.
C. Each bit of wire is then cut in two.	C.
D. Coils of wrapped wire are kept in a hot-air room.	D.
E. A machine chops the wire into lengthy pieces.	E.

Passage 2

Read the passage and then answer the questions.

Finding a Family

I hope you want to know what became of the other boys! They were waiting below to give Wendy time to explain about them, and when they had counted to five hundred they went up.

They went up by the **stair**, because they thought this would make a better **impression**. They stood in a row in front of Mrs. Darling, with their hats off, and wishing they were not wearing their pirate clothes.

They said nothing, but their eyes asked her to have them. They ought to have looked at Mr. Darling also, but they forgot about him. Of course, Mrs. Darling said at once that she would have them; but Mr. Darling was curiously sad, and they saw that he considered six a rather large number.

"I must say," he said to Wendy, "that you don't do things by halves," a **grudging** remark that the twins thought was pointed at them.

The first twin was the proud one, and he asked, with embarrassment, "Do you think we should be too much of a handful, sir? Because, if so, we can go away."

"Father!" Wendy cried, shocked; but still the cloud was on him. He knew he was behaving unworthily, but he could not help it.

"We could lie doubled up," said Nibs.

"I always cut their hair myself," said Wendy.

"George!" Mrs. Darling exclaimed, pained to see her dear one showing himself in such a poor light. Then he burst into tears, and the truth came out. He was as glad to have them as she was, he said, but he thought they should have asked his consent as well as hers, instead of treating him as a zero in his own house.

"I don't think he is a zero," Tootles cried instantly.

"Do you think he is a zero, Curly?"

"No, I don't. Do you think he is a zero, Slightly?"

"Rather not. Twin, what do you think?" It turned out that not one of them thought him a zero; and he was very pleased.

J. M. Barrie. *Peter Pan* (Kindle Locations 1848-1862).

Questions 1 and 2:

1.Which word has the same **long a** sound as *stair*?	2. How many syllables are in the word *impression*?
A. apple	A. 1
B. ant	B. 2
C. each	C. 3
D. eight	D. 4

Question 3:
Part A

Which of the following did the boys think might create a <u>bad</u> impression?

A. Going up the stairs

B. Taking their hats off

C. Wearing their pirate clothes

D. Looking at Mrs. Darling

Part B
Which of the following best supports the answer for Part A?

A. They wished they were not wearing their pirate clothes.

B. They thought they might be a handful.

C. They thought going up the stairs would make a good impression.

D. Mrs. Darling said she would have them.

Question 4: Why did Mr. Darling think he was a zero? Choose the <u>best two</u> answers.

A. The boys did not ask for his consent.

B. The boys did not like him.

C. The boys only liked Mrs. Darling.

D. The boys did not look at him.

E. The boys were a handful.

Question 5:
Part A

How many children are present in this scene?

A. 2   B. 4   C. 6   D. 8

Part B
Which of the following best supports your answer in A?

A. They saw that Mr. Darling considered six a very large number.

B. The twins thought they were talking to them.

C. The twins wanted to lie double up.

D. They said nothing but their eyes asked her to have them.

Passage 3
Read the passage below, and then answer the questions that follow.

Salmon

Eating Fish

Fish is not as **interesting** to eat as other meats. **Edible** fish are generally divided into two classes—those of white flesh and those more or less red. The red-fleshed fish have their fat distributed throughout the muscular tissues. **Salmon** is an example. In white fish, the fat is stored up in the liver so white fish is much easier to digest. White fish is also more **wholesome.**

Different kinds of fish have different health values. Their flavor and wholesomeness depend a great deal on what they eat and the water in which they live. Deep-water fish that live with strong currents are thought to be better than those found in shallow water. Fish are sometimes poisonous, owing no doubt to the food they eat.

Many persons believe fish have high value and is particularly suited to the development of the brain and nervous system. Perhaps this is because fish contain a great deal of phosphorus. **Phosphorus** is also present in the human brain, and for this reason it has been supposed that fish must be excellent **nutriment** for the brain. However, the truth is, there is no such thing as any special brain or nerve food. What is good to build up one part of the body is good for the whole body.

Science in the Kitchen / *A Scientific Treatise On Food Substances and Their Dietetic Properties, Together with a Practical Explanation of the Principles of Healthful Cookery, and a Large Number of Original, Palatable, and Wholesome Recipes* (Kindle Locations 8963-8978).

Words you may not know:
Phosphorus – a mineral that the body needs, which is found mainly in bones and teeth
Nutriment –nourishment, goodness, able to make something grow

Questions 1 and 2:

1. How many syllables are there in the word *interesting*?	2. Look at the words in the following pattern. Write one word to complete the pattern.
A. 1 B. 2 C. 3 D. 4	A. brain B. train C. drain D. strain E. _____

Questions 3 and 4:

3. What is the meaning of the word *edible* as used in the passage?
 	
    A. Not good to eat
    B. Raw
    C. Good to eat
    D. Poisonous
	4. What is the meaning of the word *wholesome*, as used in the passage?
	
	    A. Good to eat
	    B. Not good to eat
	    C. Raw
	    D. Poisonous

Question 5: The words *edible* and *wholesome* are _____.

  A. Synonyms   B. Antonyms   C. Homonyms   D. Just words

Question 6: Why is white fish much easier to digest?

  A. The fat is stored in the liver.   C. The fat is stored in the head.
  B. The fat is stored in the muscles.   D. The fat is stored in the fins.

Question 7:

What I Know	What I Want to Know	What I Learned
Fish is healthy.	What kind of fish is best to eat?	• White-flesh fish • Red-flesh fish • Fat is stored in the liver of white-flesh fish. • Fat is stored in the muscle in red-flesh fish. • There is no such thing as fish being brain food.

For this health benefit, I can eat white-meat fish.	
For this health benefit, I can eat red-meat fish.	

Evaluative Question: Based on this passage, what kind of fish do you think is best to eat and why?

Question 8: What is the author's opinion about fish? Cite evidence from the text to support your answer.

Question 9: Come up with a different title for the passage and compare your answer with a partner's.

Question 10: What questions do you have about the text? Discuss with a partner.

Passage 4

Moby Dick

"I know Captain Ahab well; I've sailed with him as mate years ago; I know what he is—a good man— not a **pious**, good man, like Bildad, but a swearing good man— something like me—only there's a good deal more of him. Aye, aye, I know that he was never very jolly; and I know that on the passage home, he was a little out of his mind for a spell; but it was the sharp shooting pains in his bleeding stump that brought that about, as any one might see.

I know, too, that ever since he lost his leg last voyage by that **accursed** whale, he's been a kind of moody—very moody, and angry sometimes; but that will all pass off. And once for all, let me tell you and assure you, young man, it's better to sail with a moody good captain than a laughing bad one.

So good-bye to you—and do not wrong Captain Ahab, because he happens to have a wicked name. Besides, my boy, he has a wife—not three voyages wedded—a sweet, resigned girl. Think of that; by that sweet girl that old man has a child: hold ye then there can be any utter, hopeless harm in Ahab? No, no, young man, Captain Ahab is a good man."

As I walked away, I was very thoughtful; what had been told to me of Captain Ahab, filled me with a certain wild **vagueness** of painfulness concerning him. And somehow, at the time, I felt sympathy and sorrow for him, but I don't know for what, unless it was the cruel loss of his leg.

And yet I also felt a strange awe of him; but that sort of awe, which I cannot at all describe, was not exactly awe; I do not know what it was. But I felt it; and it did not make me hate him though I felt uneasy at what seemed like **mystery** in him. However, other things began to occupy my thoughts and as I had other things to do for the present dark, Ahab slipped my mind.

Herman Melville. *Moby Dick; Or, The Whale* (Kindle Locations 1573-1575).

Mate – On ships, this is a title used for seamen to tell who is most senior or in charge on the ship. For example, the first mate is the office next in position to the captain. There is also a second mate and third mate.

Vocabulary

Words	Meanings
Pious	Religious, holy, godly
Accursed	Under a curse, dammed, doomed
Vagueness	Not clear, uncertain
Impatience	Restless, not patient

Question 1:

Part A

From which point of view is the story told?

   A. 1st person   B. 2nd person   C. 3rd person   D. 4th person

Part B

Which of the following best supports your answer to Part A?

   A. The writer uses "I" often.   C. The writer uses "he, she, it" often.
   B. The author uses "you" often.   D. The author uses "they" often.

How to Find the Precise Topic

In some paragraphs or readings, the precise topic is not clear. This topic is Moby Dick. But this topic seems to be very general or broad. If you examine the paragraphs, you can look for repeated words or phrases. The repeated words or phrases can point you towards a specific or precise topic. This passage talks a lot about Captain Ahab. The author felt he was a moody, swearing good man. So, the topic could be this:

Topic: Captain Ahab: a moody, swearing good man

Question 2: Which of the following best states the main idea of the reading?

   A. Captain Ahab was not liked by the person telling the story.
   B. Captain Ahab was very moody since he lost his leg.
   C. Captain Ahab had been a captain for a very long time.
   D. Although Captain Ahab was often moody and swore from the pain in his stump leg, he was a good captain.

Question 3: Identify one major supporting point and one minor supporting point. Two have already been done for you.

Major Support	Minor Support
1. He is moody and desperate and savage sometimes.	1. The mood and swearing were from pain in his leg.
2. He is newly married and has a sweet wife and child.	2. This loving captain is harmless.
3. _____	3. _____

Question 4: How did Captain Ahab lose his leg?

Cause and Effect

A *cause* is why something happened.	An *effect* is what happened.
The cause:	The effect:
_____	Captain Ahab lost his leg.

Passage 5

The Power of Rain

In various parts of England, we see evidence of the action of the <u>power</u> of rain. We observe this <u>power</u> during the present autumn in the blossoming of trees, in the flowering of primroses and other spring plants, in rich growths of **fungi**, and in various other ways. However, rain comes in season and out of season. This unseasonal rain causes a waste of the <u>power</u> of rain.

The modern theories of cause and effect show how great a loss a country suffers when there is a failure in the supply of rain, or when it rains out of its due season. When we consider rain in connection with the causes to which it is due, we begin to recognize the **enormous** amount of <u>power</u> of which the ordinary rainfall of a country represents.

We can well understand how it is that "the clouds drop fatness on the earth." The sun's heat is, of course, the main agent—we may almost say the only agent—in supplying the rainfall of a country. The process of **evaporation** carried on over large portions of the ocean's surface is continually storing up enormous masses of water in the form of invisible water vapor, ready to be **transformed** into cloud.

Then it travels for hundreds of miles across seas and continents, to be finally showered over this or that country, according to the conditions that determine the downfall of rain.

_____

Richard A. Proctor. *Light Science for Leisure Hours / A series of familiar essays on scientific subjects, natural phenomena, &c.* (Kindle Locations 2615-2620).

Study the meanings of the words given below and then reread the passage.

Words	Meanings
Fungi	A type of organism that includes molds, mildews, rusts, yeasts and mushroom plants that spring up when it is wet.
Enormous	Great or huge
Evaporation	The process of changing from liquid to vapor
Transformed	Made a thorough or dramatic change in form

Look at the Table of Contents below:

The Power of Rain
Table of Contents

Question 1: On what page does the glossary begin?

A. 5   B. 20   C. 25   D. 30

Question 2:
Part A

What does the writer say is the main agent in supplying rainfall in a country?

A. The clouds
B. The rivers
C. The moon
D. The heat of the sun

Part B
Which of the following best supports your answer to A?

A. The sun absorbs water from rivers and the ocean and stores it as water vapor.
B. The sun plays a great role in making rain.
C. The rivers are important in rainfall.
D. The clouds play an important role in rainfall.

Question 3: "This **unseasonal** rain causes a waste of the power of rain." What is the meaning of the prefix "-un" in the word "unseasonal"?

A. Out of   B. Not   C. Full of   D. Again

ANSWER KEY FOR PRACTICE EXERCISES

Lesson 2

Exercise 1

1.

Short /e/	Short /a/	Short /o/	Long /i/	Long /a/
Yes	Back	To	Rising	All
Present	That	Sobbed		Face
Yet	At	Done		Falling
Regularity	Than	Polished		Away
When	Had	Stopped		
The	And	From		
Entangled	Regularity	Possibly		
Himself	Was			
Selling	That			
Dearest	Husband			
	Having			
	Entangled			
	A			
	Man			
	Stanza			
	Instantly			
	Hand			
	Away			
	As			
	Can't			
	Understand			

2. The female character is sad and crying and her husband is trying to console her.	3. Weep- Cry Screening- To be covering Regularity-Consistency Entangled- To have become twisted together Instantly- at once	4. A suitable title will be "A Need to Weep."	5. The character is aware of her emotions and needs. She knows that she must release her emotions presently before returning to face a situation that is distressing her.

Exercise 2

1.

Sound /oi/	Sound /ea/	Sound /ee/	Sound /er/	Sound /ar/
boilers	near hear heart dreamt	sheet	after her mother never	Large

2. Mrs. Chailey is expected to sit in a cabin that is too near the boilers for her comfort and which affects her heart.	3. - Complained: expressed dissatisfaction about something - State: a condition - Inflicting: to be causing - Knew: had knowledge of - Expected: to have thought something will happen	4. A suitable title will be "Mrs. Chailey's Complaints."	5. Mrs. Vinrace is a fair woman who does not cause discomfort to others and expects everyone to do their best. She is also particular as she keeps count of the number of sheets that she has.

Exercise 3

1. D 2. C	3. Tom was a strong **swimmer**, so he was confident in the water. The **skater** stumbled and lost her balance. The **grapes** are harvested to produce wine. Adrian's house is only one **block** away from ours.	4. R-blend: trim, drip, trap, crib, fresh L-blend: plan, clap, slid, glass, black S- blend: small, snail, sky, smell, sponge

Exercise 4

1.

R-blend	S-blend	L-blend	Long - e	Long - a
Photographing Traveling From Traverse Through	Swept Past Slower Distant	Planet Fly	Receding Behind Reaches Speeds	Spacecraft Same Way Station Itinerary January Sail Range Space

| 2. The passage is about two spacecraft, Voyager 1 and Voyager 2, that captured images of the solar system. | 3. - Swept: to have moved swiftly
- Spacecraft: a machine that flies in outer space
- Encounter: an unexpected meeting
- Receding: moving back
- Itinerary: a planned route
- Exhausted: very tired
- Endless: having no end or limit | 4. A suitable title will be "The Voyagers' Journey."

5. ST- best, fast, blast
   SP- gasp, wasp, grasp |

| **Exercise 5**
1. Sting
2. Wring

Practice Exercise
1. The speaker is staring into the darkness and thinking deeply before he whispers someone's name, which is echoed back to him. | 2. - Wondering: showing curiosity
- Mortal: having to die
- Stillness: motionlessness
- Whispered: to have spoken softly
- Echo: a sound that is repeated after the original sound | 3. A suitable title will be "An Echo in the Darkness."

4. Sh- shark, wash, shrimp, publish

Ch- chase, church, coach, bench

Th- theme, than, both, path

Ph- sphere, photo, elephant, phrase | 5. The letter "k" tends to come before the letters "i" and "e" in words. The letter "c" comes before the letters "a," "o" and "u." |

LESSON 3
Exercise 1

1. Long /a/	2. Verbs		3. Verbs	
d<u>a</u>te	<u>grin</u>	<u>cling</u>	<u>blink</u>	<u>drip</u>
g<u>a</u>te	<u>bit</u>	<u>fling</u>	<u>drink</u>	<u>flip</u>
gr<u>a</u>te	<u>fit</u>	<u>ring</u>	<u>link</u>	<u>grip</u>
pl<u>a</u>te	<u>hit</u>	<u>sing</u>	<u>sink</u>	<u>ship</u>
r<u>a</u>te	<u>knit</u>	<u>wring</u>	<u>stink</u>	<u>drain</u>
st<u>a</u>te	<u>quit</u>	<u>bill</u>	<u>think</u>	<u>gain</u>
	<u>split</u>	<u>drill</u>	<u>chip</u>	<u>delay</u>
			<u>dip</u>	<u>play</u>

Exercise 2	Exercise 3
-ack: attack, rack, sack, snack	1. **Ball-** The pedestrian returned the ball to the kid.
	2. **Mall-** The mall will be closing in one hour.
-eat: neat, treat, seat, meat	3. **Game-** We watched the game by Macy's house.
	4. **Blame-** The employer shifted the blame to one of his employees.
-ice: rice, slice, twice, lice	5. **Crop-** The instructions stated to chop the vegetables first.
	6. **Joke-** The audience found the joke to be insensitive.
-ick: pick, sick, trick, click	7. **Spoke-** After I spoke with the lawyer, I made my decision.

Exercise 4

1. Dump- To throw away something *People often dump their garbage in rivers.* **Plump-** Being rounded in shape *We got a plump chicken for our meal.* **Paw-** an animal's foot *The dog rested his paw on David's leg in hopes of getting a treat.* **Stuck-** to have been unable to move *The ring was stuck on her swollen finger.* **Snug-** to be comfortable and warm *Marie looked quite snug by the fireside.*	**2. Pale-** to have little colour *Santiago looked quite pale before his presentation.* **Stale-** to be no longer fresh *The impoverished family often ate stale bread.* **Pest-** a destructive animal *We called the company upon realizing we had a pest problem.* **Nest-** a place where a bird lays eggs and shelter its young *A bird's nest, containing two fledglings, fell out the tree.* **Clock-** a device that measures time *The ticking of the clock irritated Wendell during the exam.*

Exercise 5	Exercise 6		2. **Words with Prefixes**	Dreaming
A. Impolite	1.		Unbroken	Dreams
B. Unsafe	a. Rubbed	b. Rubbing		Dared
C. Recharged	c. Fixed	d. Fixing		Stillness
D. Misbehaved	e. Jogged	f. Jogging	**Words with Suffixes**	Spoken
	g. Hopped	h. Hopping	Darkness	Whispered
	i. Picked	j. Picking	Peering	Murmured
			Wondering	Merely
			Fearing	
			Doubting	

TABE 11 & 12 CONSUMABLE STUDENT READING MANUAL FOR LEVEL E

Practice Exercise	Ma-nage-ment	Pro-fess-or	En-vi-ro-nment
	A-ssess-ment	A-ca-de-my	In-ter-pre-ta-tion
Col-lege	En-roll-ment	E-co-no-mic	Me-thod
A-na-ly-sis	App-li-ca-tion	Li-bra-ry	Po-li-cy
U-ni-ver-si-ty	Tu-i-tion	Com-po-si-tion	Pro-ce-dure
Spe-ci-fic	Re-sponse	Dis-ser-ta-tion	Theo-ry
A-re-a	In-for-ma-tive	Re-search	Sig-ni-fi-cant

LESSON 4
Practice Exercise
1. The darkness and echoes in a cave come to mind when I read the text.

2. The text reminds me of the loneliness and heartbreak many people experience every day.

LESSON 5
Exercise 1
A, B

Exercise 2
Picture 1- D
Picture 2- B or D
Picture 3- A
Picture 4- B

Exercise 3
Picture 1- The building is old and unkempt so no one might have been living in it or utilizing it for years.

Picture 2- The athlete has prosthetic legs and he is competing in a race. Therefore, he mut be competing in the Paralympic Games or another sporting event for persons with disabilities.

LESSON 6
Exercise 1
1. B
2. B
3. C
4. The Fourth of July is the most popular day for grilling in the United States. Moreover, the child is holding a United States flag, which implies that the group is celebrating Independence Day.

Exercise 2
1. C
2. B

LESSON 7
Exercise 1
1. C
2. A

Exercise 2
1. B
2. A

LESSON 8
Literal
4. There are 4 people.

Inferential
1. No, the dog is not happy.
2. Its ears are drooping and its face is angled downwards.
3. No, I do not think the dog likes to be bathed.

4. I believe so many of them are washing the dog because they would like to finish quickly. It may also be because he is very dirty and it is taking a lot of effort to get out all the dirt.

Evaluative
1. They could have taken his favorite toy to the bath with him or only allow one person to bathe him whom he is comfortable with.
2. No, I do not think he is bathed often because many people are bathing him, which could indicate that he is very dirty.
3. I will bathe my dog once every week.

LESSON 9
1. B
2. C

LESSON 10
1. C
2. B
3. No, I do not support the hunting of wild animals because each animal plays an important role in balancing nature. For example, the overhunting of one species can lead to the overpopulation of another.
(Answers may vary.)

LESSON 12
Exercise 1
1. Next, afterwards, now, before, then, suddenly, meanwhile
2. E, A, C, D, B, F
3. Topic: C
4. Part A: D
   Part B: B, E

Exercise 2
1. 4 stages

2. egg, caterpillar, chrysalis, butterfly

3. First, next, finally

Exercise 3

B, A, D, C, F, E

Exercise 4
6. People died
7. Loss of electricity

Exercise 5
Causes: diet, cycling, drinking water, weight training

Exercise 6
1. B
2. A
3. A

LESSON 13
Practice Exercise

1. Third-person point of view

2. Third-person point of view

3. a. Clues: "If ever I see" and "I must not, in play."
b. I
c. First-person point of view

4. a. Clue: "Where are you going, you little pig?"
b. You
c. Second-person point of view

LESSON 14

1. 30%.

2. Seventy-five (75)

3. 100%

Practice Exercise

1. Title – Our Favorite Animals
2. A. Horizontal label – Animals
   B. Vertical label – Number of children
3. Scale- 2
4. Favorite animal – Dog
   Least favorite – Horse

Longer Selections

Passage 1 – Needle-town
1. D
2. B
3. Topic – D
4. Part A – B
   Part B – B and E
5. B
6. Order of the story
   D, E, A, B, C
 	
Passage 2 – Finding a Family
1. D
2. C
3. Part A – C
   Part B – A
4. Best two – A & D
5. Part A – C
   Part B – A
	Passage 3 – Eating Fish
	1. D
	2. chain, gain, main
	3. C
	4. A
	5. A
	6. A
	
	7. White-meat fish benefits-
	easier to digest, more
	wholesome and has phosphorus
	Red-meat fish benefits- has
	phosphorus
		Evaluative answer: white fish is best to eat as it is easier to digest and is more wholesome than red fish.
		
		8. The author does not think fish is interesting as he states, "Fish is not as **interesting** to eat as other meats."
		
		9. Another title is "The Benefits of fish."

Passage 4 – Moby Dick
1. Part A – A
   Part B – A
2. D
3. Major support-He is a good captain.
   Minor support- He was a little out of his mind for a period.
4. Cause- Captain Ahab lost his leg because he was bitten by a whale.
	Passage 5 – The Power of Rain
	1. D
	2. Part A – D
	   Part B – A
	3. B

READING SKILLS SELF-EVALUATION

Mastery of Reading Strategy Skills		Often	Sometimes	Never
Phonics	I can decode English words or break them into sound parts.			
Pre-reading	I can preview the text by skimming and setting a purpose for reading.			
Pre-reading	I can set a purpose for reading by making predictions.			
Pre-reading	I can use my background knowledge to connect to what I am reading.			
During reading	I can figure out the main idea of a text.			
During reading	I can ask myself questions about the text.			
During reading	I can use visualization to make meaning.			
During reading	I can monitor my comprehension.			
During reading	I can monitor my understanding and use fix-up strategies like rereading.			
During reading	I can use context clues to guess the meaning of words.			
During reading	I can infer meaning while reading a text.			
During reading	I can identify and determine meaning of figurative language like similes, metaphors and personification.			
During reading	I can identify text structures and use the information to help me remember what I read.			
Post-reading	I can summarize the main point and key details in a text.			
Post-reading	I can relate information to myself and the world.			
Post-reading	I can determine the theme of a story or poem.			
Post-reading	I can explain events based on what happened and why.			
Post-reading	I can write an entry in my Reflective Journal.			

ASSESSMENT

READING PRACTICE TEST

PART I

You are required to read the 4 passages and answer the 24 questions.

Your test time will be 2.5 minutes per question.

Your total time for this test is one hour (60 minutes).

Read the following passages and answer the questions.

Passage 1

The Honey-Bee

This is a very curious, and remarkably **industrious** little insect. We thank this insect for one of the most tasty and wholesome sweets that nature makes. This sweet is one of the best things that the promised-land is said to be full of.

In every hive of bees, there are three kinds of bees. Each **colony** has a single queen, hundreds of male drones, and thousands of laborers. Queens lay fertilized eggs, and can lay 2,000 eggs in a day.

The laborers or worker bees are by far the greatest number. They are all female. The job of the laborers is to look for food, store honey for winter and build honey-combs. Drones are male honey-bees. Their job is to fertilize new queens. Drones die soon after mating. When the weather begins to get cold, the laborers will drive the drones that are left, from the hive. Since they have not worked in the summer, they must not eat in winter.

If bees are looked at through a glass hive, all appears at first like confusion: but, on a more careful look, every bee has a job to do. When you are outside in the spring or summer, look at the trees. When the trees are in bloom, you will be sure to see the busy bees and to hear their busy hum.

Unknown. *The History of Insects* (Kindle Locations 113-116).

A **colony** – The family unit of bees made up of a queen, workers and drones

Question 1: What is the <u>best</u> answer?

We thank the bee for a <u>wholesome sweet</u> that nature makes.

What is the wholesome sweet?

A. Milk

B. Honeycomb

C. Honey

D. Honey-butter

Question 2: Which is the <u>best</u> answer?

The promised land (heaven) was said to abound or be full of the "wholesome sweet" and what other food?

A. Milk   B. Honeycomb   C. Honey-butter   D. Honey

Question 3:

Part A
Which of the following is the <u>best</u> meaning of the word *industrious*?

A. Hard-working

B. Lazy

C. Working sometimes

D. Not working at all

Part B
Which of the following sentences <u>best</u> supports your answer to A?

A. In every hive there are three kinds of bees.

B. The job of the laborers is to look for food.

C. Every bee has a job to do.

D. Drones are male honey-bees.

Question 4: Study the following table of contents.

HISTORY OF INSECTS

Table of Contents	Page
The History of Insects	10
Grasshoppers	12
Crickets	14
Locusts	16
Scorpions	18
Honey-Bees	21
Spiders	23
Glossary	25
Index	27

On which page would you find the "Honey-Bee?"

A. Page 10   B. Page 21   C. Page 14   D. Page 27

Question 5: Look at the table of contents. On which page would you find the glossary?

A. Page 16   B. Page 18   C. Page 25   D. Page 27

Question 6:

Part A
Which of the following is the correct answer? The beginning sounds in "sweet," /sw/, is an example of a

A. Consonant blend

B. Consonant digraph

C. Vowel digraph

D. Diphthong

Sweets – jelly beans in a jar

Part B

Which of the following reasons supports your answer to Part A?

A. The vowels combine to make one sound.

B. The sound glides from one vowel to the next.

C. Each sound is heard in the blend.

D. Two consonants blend to make one sound.

Passage 2

The Gentle Monster

"This is Achilles," she said.

She had her hand on the head of the great **monster.** "He is as gentle and kind as a kitten. But he looks as if he could **swallow** us alive. Don't touch him but stand still and let him sniff you all over. It is his way of getting to know you."

The boy obeyed. He did not move. The panting jaws and moist black nose of the dog came nearer. He could feel the dog's hot breath on his hands, face, and hair. Then the **quivering** nose moved over his clothing. After a long time, the brown eyes met his and he whispered softly, "Achilles!" The dog wagged his tail.

"You do not need to be afraid of him now," said Mrs. Jones.

"The **Terriers** are Jack Horner and Boy Blue. And the **Akita**, Miss Nancy's dog, is called Rags." Sensing that he was being talked about, the dog blinked with friendly eyes at Walter through its mop of coarse white hair.

"In the other pen," continued Mrs. Jones, "are the **Pekingese** pups and I shall expect you to take the best of care of them.

They are fussy little creatures and very valuable. I, myself, however, care very little for the money value of a dog. It is the lovable traits it has that interest me. I should adore wee **Lola,** here, if she were not worth a cent.

However, Mr. Jones likes to own blue ribbon dogs and enter them at the shows. Therefore, I will tell you that **Lola, Mimi, and Fifi,**" as she spoke she pointed out the dogs in question, "cost quite a lot of money and their loss or illness would hurt us a lot."

So you must follow the directions concerning them most carefully. And if you do not understand something about them, come to me at once." As she spoke she often looked at the boy beside her with a quick, bright smile.

Sara Ware Bassett. *Walter and the Wireless* (Kindle Locations 873-877)

Question 7: Which word has a **short** "e" vowel sound?

A. He

B. Need

C. Wee

D. Head

Question 8:
Part A
What is the <u>main idea</u> of the passage?

A. The dog liked the boy who was to care for them.

B. The boy had his first day on the job.

C. The boy's job was to take care of Achilles and the other dogs.

D. The boy loved dogs.

Part B
Which <u>two sentences</u> support the answer to Part A?

A. The dog liked the boy who was to care for them.

B. You must follow the directions concerning them most carefully.

C. I shall expect you to take the best care of them.

D. You do not need to be afraid of him now.

E. Mr. Jones likes to own blue ribbon dogs.

Question 9:
Part A
Why was the boy told to stand still?

A. So the dog would not bite him

B. So the dog could sniff him and get to know him

C. So the dog could lick him

D. So the dog could kiss him

Part B
Which two of the following best support your answer to A?

A. The dog smelled his hands, face, hair and clothing.

B. After smelling him, the dog looked at the boy and wagged his tail.

C. The dog liked the boy.

D. The dog looked fearsome.

E. The dog was tame.

Question 10:
Part A
How many dogs were there in all?

A. 5   B. 6   C. 7   D. 8

Part B
How do you know? <u>Select two</u> of the following that name the dogs.

A. There were Achilles, the two terriers, and the Akita.

B. There was Achilles and Lola.

C. There were Lola, Mimi, and Fifi.

D. There were Jack Horner and Boy Blue.

E. There was Achilles and the Akita.

Question 11: Put the following in sequence order: What happened first, next and last.
The first one is done for you.

C. The boy stood still.	

Question 12:
Part A
Divide the word *quivering* into its syllables or sound parts. How many syllables does the word have?

A. 1   B. 2   C. 3   D. 4

Part B
How many claps would you get?

A. 1   B. 2   C. 3   D. 4

Passage 3

The Importance of Water

Percent of Water Contained in Items	
World	75%
Fruits	80%
The human br	75%

1. Water is a very important part of the makeup of the earth and the solar system. Three quarters of the weight of the world is water. Water is also an important part of most rocks.

2. Fruits and vegetables contain water. Some vegetables are 97 percent water. Fruits are about 80 percent water.

3. Fully three-fourths or 75 percent of the weight of our bodies is water. Man has been described as consisting merely of a few pounds of solid matter distributed through six buckets of water.

4. Water enters the **tissues** of vegetable and animal matter. The health of an individual family or community depends on the purity of the water supply.

5. Water is needed for domestic purposes. Water is used indoors and outdoors. We use water for cooking, bathing, washing and gardening. It is also needed for mechanical and heating purposes. It is needed for planting and growing crops and in business.

6. Your brain depends on having a lot of water. Water gives your brain the energy to do its functions of thinking and memory. Indeed, the power that moves the world, the human brain, is 75 percent water.

_____

McCurdy, C. W. (Charles W.). 1894. *Water and water analysis. Moscow, Idaho: University of Idaho, Agricultural Experiment Station* (Digital Library of America).

13. Which word has a **long "e"** vowel sound?

A. Have   B. Three   C. Some   D. Use

14. Look at the table "Percent of Water Contained in Certain Items." Which section of the table supports the information in paragraph six of the passage?

A. World   B. Fruits   C. Our bodies   D. Human brain

15.
Part A
What is the main idea of the article?

A. Water is a main part of the world and everything in it.
B. Fruits and vegetables are made up of a great deal of water.
C. The brain is made up of a great deal of water.
D. Water is needed in life.

Part B
Which sentence supports the answer to A?

A. Water is needed for irrigation and commercial use.
B. Water is used indoor and outdoor.
C. Water is needed for domestic purposes.
D. Water is a very important part of the earth and the solar system.

16. Read the sentence. Say the underlined word.
"Three quarters of the weight of the world is water."

Choose the word with the same blend sound as the first three letters of the underlined word.

A. Thumbs   B. Thread   C. Tree   D. Thirteen

17. What is the meaning of the word "tissues" as used in the following sentence?
   "Water enters into the **tissues** of vegetable and animal matter."

   A. Body parts or cells
   B. Living persons

   C. Animals
   D. Tissue paper

18.
Part A
Read the sentence. Say the underlined word.

   "Water is a very <u>important</u> part of the makeup of the earth and the solar system."

How many syllables are in the word *important*?

   A. 1   B. 2   C. 3   D. 4

Part B
How many claps would you get?

   A. 1   B. 2   C. 3   D. 4

Passage 4

Iron and Metals

Metals are made from **ores** or a met[al] bearing mineral or rock, that can be dug [out] of the earth. These ores are found in ma[ny] parts of the world. Iron is the m[ost] **common**, as well as the most useful metal[.]

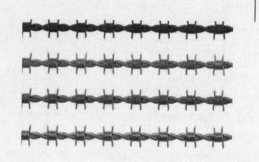

Many things we use are made of iron. The steel tha[t is used to make our knives, tools and] other things are made from iron. Iron is largely used for making bridges, railings, fire-grates and hammers.

Lead, copper, tin and zinc are metals also. So are silver and gold. Men must dig deep down into the earth to find them. The holes and passages that they make are called mines.

All metals are heavy. All will melt in great heat, and all can be hammered out into thin sheets or drawn out into wire.

Various. *Chambers's Elementary Science Readers* / Book I (Kindle Locations 1388-1395).

19. Read the sentence. Say the underlined word.
    "Iron is the most <u>common</u> metal."

Choose the word that means the <u>opposite</u> of the underlined word.

A. Ordinary
B. Exact

C. Uncommon
D. Important

20.
Part A
What is an **ore?** Choose the <u>best</u> answer.

A. Ore is a mineral or rock from which a valuable substance can be dug out.
B. Ore is something in the earth.

C. Ore is something that has been in the earth for a long time.
D. Ore is something valuable.

Part B
What kind of vocabulary clue is given in the following sentence?

"Metals are made from **ores,** or a metal-bearing mineral or rock, that can be dug out of the earth."

A. Synonym
B. Antonym
C. Example
D. Restatement

21.
Part A
What is the most common or useful metal?

A. Gold
B. Silver
C. Copper
D. Iron

Part B
Which sentence supports the answer to Part A?

A. Iron is the most common as well as the most useful metal.
B. Metals are found in many parts of the world.

C. All metals are heavy.
D. Many things we use are made of metals.

22. How are metals found?

A. Many are found lying on top of the earth.
B. Men must dig deep down into the earth to find them.

C. Metals are found in stores.
D. Metals are found in homes.

23. What are mines?

    A. Mines are holes and passages dug to find metals.
    B. Mines are where a lot of people work.

    C. Mines are in the earth.
    D. Mines can be gold, silver or bronze.

24.
Part A
Choose the best answer. Which of the following is the main idea of the reading?

    A. Iron dug out of the earth is used to make many items.
    B. People depend a great deal on iron.

    C. Iron comes from mines.
    D. Without iron, we would be lost.

Part B
Which two sentences best supports your answer for A.

    A. Many things we use are made of iron.
    C. Our knives and tools are made of iron.
    D. Bridges are made of iron.

    B. Iron is the most common or most useful metal.
    E. Silver and gold are metals.

ASSESSMENT

READING PRACTICE TEST

PART II

You are required to read 4 passages and answer the 24 questions assigned.

Your test time will be 2.5 minutes per question.

Your total time for this test is one hour (60 minutes)

Passage 1

Recycling Paper

"It is such a wet day, I don't know what to do!" said Harry, looking very unhappy.

"Are you tired of your drawing and painting?" asked his mother.

"Oh yes! And we have played at houses, and had the bricks out on the floor, and now there is nothing to do, and it is not nearly dinnertime yet. Will you read to us, Mother?"

"Not just now! But if you would help me a little I should get on faster, and then we might have a nice time before dinner."

"Great," cried Harry. He ran to the foot of the stairs and called Dora. Down came Dora very fast, with her doll in her arms, and the dog at her heels.

"What I want you to do," said mother, "is to tear up these old papers and put them into this trash bag. The man is coming soon to take it to the paper-mill."

"Why is it taken to the paper-mill?" asked Harry.

"To be made over again into paper. Perhaps it will come back to us some day, very clean. Or it may be made into a newspaper, and Father may bring it home in his pocket."

"Or we may get it in copy-books at school."

"Yes, or it may come from the shop with rice in it."

"It may never come at all," said Dora. "Perhaps it will go to some other house."

"That is quite likely," said mother, who was now cleaning the **fireplace**. They went on putting the paper into the trash bag for a long time.

Then Harry asked, "How was paper made before there was old paper to make it of?"

"Oh, it is not made of paper only. It is made of old rags, old ropes"—— Harry and Dora began to laugh. "And **straw**, and wood, and a kind of grass." ——

"Now, are you joking, Mother?"

"No, indeed! They cut the wood and straw into tiny bits, and they cut and tear the rags and boil them."

"And what do they do with the grass?"

"They put it into a machine, which makes it into paper."

Various. *Chambers's Elementary Science Readers* / Book I (Kindle Location 965-991

1. Which word has a **long /a/** vowel sound?

    A. What   B. Harry   C. Dora   D. Day

2.
Part A
How many syllables are in the word <u>fireplace</u>?

    A. 1   B. 2   C. 3   D. 4

Part B
How many claps would you get?

    A. 1   B. 2   C. 3   D. 4

3. Read the sentence. Say the underlined word.

"And <u>straw</u> and wood and a kind of grass," Dora said.

Choose the word with the <u>same blend sound</u> as the <u>first three letters</u> of the underlined word.

    A. Stamp   B. Steam   C. Stream   D. Sting

4.
Part A
What is the main idea of the reading?

    A. Even wood and straw went into paper recycling.
    B. In the past, paper was recycled differently than it is today.
    C. Paper recycling is very important.
    D. We should recycle old paper.

Part B
Which two sentences best support your answer to Part A?

    A. Paper was made of old rags, old rope, grass and old paper.
    B. The man is coming soon to take it to the paper mill.
    C. Even wood and straw went into paper recycling.
    D. It is made over again into paper.
    E. They put the paper into the trash bags.

5.
Part A
From which point of view is the story told?

    A. 1st person   B. 2nd person   C. 3rd person   D. 4th person

Part B

Which of the following best supports your answer to A?

A. The writer uses "I" often.

B. The author uses "you" often.

C. The writer uses "he, she, it" often.

D. The author uses "they" often.

6. The prefix "re-" means "back or again." Which of the words below means "To be <u>made over again</u>"?

A. Repeat

B. Return

C. Retry

D. Remake

Passage 2

Knocked Unconscious

Get out of the way, or I'll push you off the road!" threatened Tom, calmly.

'll not go until I get ready," said Andy.

Oh, yes you will," said our hero quietly. He drove his ar ahead slowly. It was within a few feet of the rriage containing Andy. The bully had dropped his

3

Tom made his plans. He saw that the horse was a quiet, **sl**eepy one, that would not run away, no matter what happened, and he only intended to gently push the horse carriage to one side, and pass on. The front of his auto came up against the side of the horse carriage.

"Here, you stop!" cried Andy, angrily.

4

"It's too late now," answered Tom, grimly.

Andy reached for the horsewhip. Tom put on a little more power, and the carriage began to **sl**ide across the road, but the old horse never opened his eyes.

5

"Take that!" cried Andy, raising his whip, with the intention of hitting Tom across the face, for the front of the auto was open. But the blow never fell. The next instant, the car gave a lurch as one of the wheels **sl**id against a stone, and, as Andy was standing up, and leaning forward, he was thrown forward by his head and fell into the road.

6

"Oh, dear, I hope I haven't hurt him!" said Tom, as he leaped from his auto. Tom bent over the bully. There was a little cut on Andy's forehead, and his face was white. He had been knocked out because of his meanness. However, Tom was frightened. He lifted Andy's head on his arm, and brushed back his hair. Andy was unconscious.

Victor Appleton. *Tom Swift and His Wireless Message* (Kindle Locations 248-259).

120

7. Which word has a **long /o/** vowel sound?

A. Stop
B. Drop
C. Note
D. Out

8.
Part A
Which of the following is the effect? What happened?

Choose the <u>best</u> answer that tells what happened to Andy.

A. Andy fell headfirst into the road.
B. Andy was standing up and leaning forward.
C. Andy tried to hit Tom with a whip.
D. The car lurched forward.

Part B
Why did it happen?

A. The front of the auto was open.
B. Andy was driving the horse carriage.
C. The wheels hit a stone, and the car moved forward.
D. Andy was standing up and leaning forward.

9.
Part A
How many syllables are in the word *containing*?

A. 1
B. 2
C. 3
D. 4

Part B
How many claps would you get?

A. 1
B. 2
C. 3
D. 4

10. Say the following words.

Leaped, sleep, feet, lead, deep

These words are all examples of which of the following?

A. Consonant blend
B. Consonant digraph
C. Vowel digraph
D. Diphthong

11.
Part A
Andy was knocked unconscious. How did Tom feel about this?

A. Tom felt Andy deserved it.
B. Tom felt Andy was responsible.
C. Tom was afraid.
D. Tom was happy.

Part B

Which two sentences best supports your answer at A?

A. "Oh, dear, I hope I haven't hurt him!" said Tom.
B. He had been knocked out because of his meanness.
C. Tom was frightened.
D. He lifted Andy's head and brushed back his hair.
E. Tom bent over the bully.

12. The words *slide, slid, slowly* and *sleepy* are all examples of which of the following?

A. Consonant digraphs
B. Consonant blends

C. Diphthongs
D. Vowel digraphs

Passage 3

The Reunion

At the stroke of seven, Uncle Bob Cabot presented himself at the University Club, where Uncle Tom Curtis was waiting for him, and the two men held hands warmly. How big Uncle Tom Curtis looked and, how rosy and how clean! And what a nice smile he had!

A gondola is a flat-bottomed Venetian rowing boat, similar to a canoe.
The **prow** is the front part of the ship's bow that cuts through the water.

The dinner was very good. The filet was done to a turn, and there was just enough seasoning on the mushrooms. As for the grilled potatoes, even Hannah herself couldn't have improved upon them. An old Harvard "grad" came over from the next table and greeted Uncle Tom Curtis, telling him he did not look a day older than when he was in college. Although he had gray hairs Uncle Tom Curtis seemed to believe it.

Then they talked of the last Harvard boat race, the old professors and things they did back then. After the other man had left, the waiter brought coffee and cheese. Uncle Tom Curtis seemed to have no end of stories at which Uncle Bob Cabot laughed until he was very red in the face. Then, Uncle Bob told some stories and Uncle Tom Curtis sat back in his chair and laughed. He wiped his eyes and mopped his forehead.

Then Uncle Bob said that of course the Club was all very well. However, at the hour set, the gondola glided up to the steps of the Grand Canal Hotel. Jean and Hannah were waiting. It was an unusually beautiful gondola. It had scarlet curtains and a gold prow carved in the shape of a woman's head.

Jean jumped forward, eagerly, her eyes on the magic boat. Then, suddenly, her foot slipped on the slime left by the tide on the marble step. She would have fallen into the water, but a young boy quickly leaped forward and caught her. Hannah, white with fright, took the girl in her arms.

"Oh, my dear child!" she wailed. "My precious lamb! Thank goodness, you are safe. Think if you'd been drowned before you had had a chance to see Venice at all! But you are quite safe now, honey.

Don't be frightened. Young man," and she turned to the boy, "that was a good deed of yours. What is your name? But there—how silly to be asking him when he can't understand a word I'm saying.

I forgot no one could understand anything in this queer, upside-down town where the streets are water when they ought to be land."

_____

Sara Ware Bassett. The Story of Glass (Kindle Locations 326-331).

13. Which word has a **long /i/** vowel sound?

A. Magic   B. Until   C. Dinner   D. Nice

14.
Part A
Which of the following is the <u>main idea</u> of the reading? Choose the <u>best</u> answer.

A. The reunion dinner was very tasty.
B. Uncle Tom Curtis and Uncle Bob Cabot had an enjoyable reunion.

C. The Venice reunion was lovely, but then the child fell into the water.
D. They planned a gondola ride.

Part B
Which two sentences best support your answer to A?

A. The dinner was good.
B. Jean jumped forward eagerly, her eyes on the magic boat.
C. The young boy saved the child from falling into the water.
D. That was a good deed of yours.
E. Then they told of the last Harvard boat race.

15.
Part A
From which point of view is the story told?

A. 1st person   B. 2nd person   C. 3rd person   D. 4th person

Part B
Which of the following best supports your answer to Part A?

A. The writer uses "I" often.
B. The author uses "you" often.

C. The writer uses "he, she, it" often.
D. The author uses "they" often.

16. Which college did the men attend?

    A. Columbia   B. Harvard   C. Yale   D. Temple

17. Read the following sentence.

"Young man," she said and turned to the **boy.**

The word "boy" is an example of a

    A. Consonant digraph   C. Diphthong
    B. Consonant blend   D. Vowel digraph

18. Which of the following is the reading's text structure or organizational pattern?

    A. Compare and contrast   C. Time-order
    B. Sequence pattern   D. Cause and effect

EGGS and Nutriments

1. As will be seen from the analysis given below, an egg is very rich in nutrients. It is indeed one of the most highly concentrated forms of a food rich in nutrients. About one-third of the weight of an egg is filled with solid nutriment.

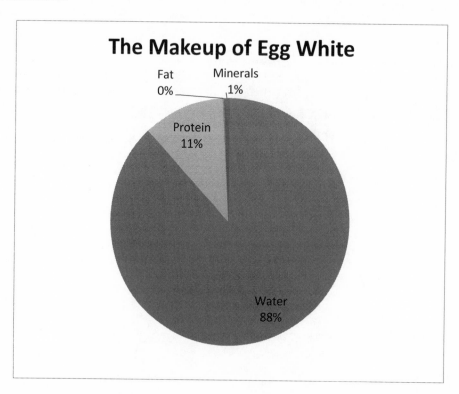

The Makeup of Egg White

Fat 0%
Minerals 1%
Protein 11%
Water 88%

2. The white or albumen of the egg is made up mainly of water in a dissolved state, covered in layers of thin membrane. When beaten, the membranes are broken. The white, because it is filled with **gluten,** a glue like elastic substance, becomes tangled and retains air and gets fluffy.

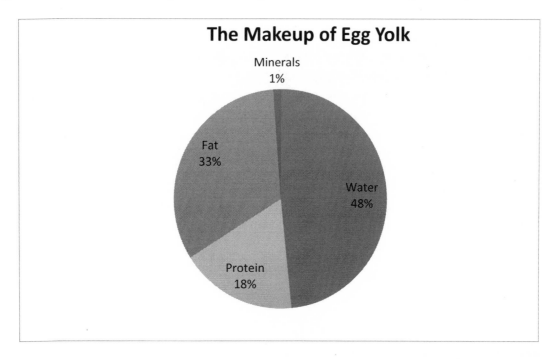

3. The yolk is yellow in color and contains all the fatty matter. It is covered in a thin film of cells, which separates it from the surrounding white. The yolk, being lighter than the white, floats to that portion of the egg that is at the top. It is held in position by two cords, one from each end of the egg.

4. The average weight of an egg is about two ounces. Ten per cent is shell, sixty percent is white, and thirty percent is yolk. Because of its nutrients, the egg is a good food to be served in cases of sickness. The patient can secure a large amount of nourishment in small doses from eating eggs.

E. E. Kellogg. *Science in the Kitchen / A Scientific Treatise On Food Substances and Their Dietetic Properties, Together with a Practical Explanation of the Principles of Healthful Cookery, and a Large Number of Original, Palatable, and Wholesome Recipes* (Kindle Locations 8461-8476).

19. Which word has a **long /o/** vowel sound?

A. Good
B. Color
C. From
D. Food

20.
Part A
What is the main idea of the article?

A. As a food, eggs are extremely rich in nutrients.

B. People who are ill should eat a lot of eggs.

C. Even the shell of the egg is rich in nutrients.

D. The yolk of the egg has a lot of fat.

Part B
Which two sentences support the answer to Part A?

A. The white or albumen of the egg is made up mainly of water.
B. The egg is a good food to be served in cases of sickness.
C. The white of the egg is made up mainly of albumen.
D. The egg is one of the most highly concentrated forms of food rich in nutrients.
E. The average weight of an egg is about two ounces.

21. Look at the first pie chart, "The Makeup of Egg White." Which section of the pie chart most clearly supports the information in paragraph 2?

A. The section of the pie chart labeled "fat."
B. The section of the pie chart labeled "minerals."
C. The section of the pie chart labeled "water."
D. The section of the pie chart labeled "protein."

22. Look at the second pie chart, "The Makeup of Egg Yolk." How much fat does the egg yolk contain?

A. 48 percent   B. 1 percent   C. 18 percent   D. 33 percent

23. What is the meaning of *gluten*as, as used in the following sentence?

"The albumen, because it is filled with **gluten**, a glue-like, elastic substance, becomes tangled and retains air and gets fluffy."

Part A

A. A glue-like, elastic substance
B. A fatty substance
C. A watery substance
D. An egg substance

Part B
What type of context clue is used in the sentence?

A. Synonym   B. Antonym   C. Example   D. Definition

24. What percent of the egg is a shell?

A. 60%   B. 10%   C. 30%   D. 2%

ANSWER KEYS

TEST 1

Passage 1 The Honey-Bee	Passage 2 The Gentle Monster	Passage 3 The Importance of Water	Passage 4 Iron and Metals
1. C	7. D	13. B	19. C
2. A	8. Part A – C	14. D	20. Part A – A
3. Part A – A	Part B – B, C	15. Part A – A	Part B – C
Part B – C	9. Part A – B	Part B – D	21. Part A – D
4. B	Part B – A, B	16. B	Part B – A
5. C	10. Part A – C	17. A	22. B
6. Part A – A	Part B – A, C	18. Part A – C	23. A
Part B – C	11. C, B, A, D, E	Part B – C	24. Part A – A
	12. Part A – C		Part B – A, B
	Part B – C		

TEST 2

Passage 1 Recycling Paper	Passage 2 Knocked Unconscious	Passage 3 The Reunion	Passage 4 Eggs and Nutriments
1. D	7. C	13. D	19. D
2. Part A – B	8. Part A – A	14. Part A – C	20. Part A – A
Part B – B	Part B – C	Part B – A, C	Part B – B, D
3. C	9. Part A – C	15. Part A – C	21. C
4. Part A – B	Part B – C	Part A – C	22. D
Part B – A, C	10. C	16. B	23. Part A– A
5. Part A – C	11. Part A – C	17. C	Part B – D
Part B – C	Part B – A, C	18. C	24. B
6. D	12. B		

ABOUT COACHING FOR BETTER LEARNING, LLC

CBL helps develop systems that increase performance and save time, resources and energy.

If you identify typos and errors in the text, please let us know at teamcbl@coachingforbetterlearning.com. We promise to fix them and send you a free copy of the updated textbook to thank you.

Made in the USA
Columbia, SC
29 April 2024

35050532R00079